Real Estate Acquisition

150 Techniques for Serious Investors

William Tappan

Real Estate Acquisition
150 Techniques for Serious Investors

ISBN 13: 978-1479102938
ISBN 10: 1479102938

Edited by Molly and Jim Cameron of Cameron Editorial Services
mj.edit@cox.net

Thanks to Alli Von Mohr for bringing the cover together.

This publication is designed to provide accurate and authoritative information in regard to the subject matter covered. It is sold with the understanding that neither the author nor the publisher is engaged in rendering legal, accounting, securities trading or other professional services. If legal or financial advice or services or other expert assistance is required, the services of a competent professional person should be sought.
—From a declaration of principles jointly adopted by a committee of the American Bar Association and a committee of publishers and associations

Books by William Tappan
Real Estate Exchange and Acquisition Techniques (1978)
The Real Estate Acquisition Handbook (1979)
Real Estate Exchange & Acquisition Techniques (1989)
Handbook for the Financial Analysis of Real Estate Investments (1993)
Real Estate Acquisition (2012)
The 7 Laws of Real Estate: A Guide for New Investors (2013)

Contents

Preface

When I started investing in real estate decades ago, my first stop was a book store to find information on the various techniques to finance and acquire real estate. With little money and less experience, I knew the right book would help. There was no such thing available. *Real Estate Acquisition* is the book I couldn't find. I had to learn the hard way, making my own mistakes and storing experiences, while relying on my mentors and colleagues who had been through the learning process before me. They were kind and generous people to whom I will always be grateful. My hope is that their helping hands will be usefully reflected on the pages that follow.

This book is designed to help you acquire real estate for financial security. It is composed of specific techniques to cut through problems and make real estate ownership part of your life. Often it is simply a process of looking at a specific property in a new way. For example, are you considering the personal circumstances of the owner? Owners tend to be more cooperative when the structure of the transaction meets their interests. Looked at in this light, acquisition becomes an exercise in structuring and explaining how your offer meshes with the underlying interests of the seller, which are not always easy to understand.

A cash purchase is only one of the hundreds of ways to acquire real estate. Many of the most effective techniques rely entirely on terms worked out with property owners who don't even want an immediate large cash payment. Every seller has personal interests and objectives, which sometimes far outweigh the cold financial terms of a transaction. When understood, they can be a source of flexibility that increases the likelihood of success. Understanding the motives and negotiating with owners is the primary challenge of a real estate acquisition strategy. Fortunately, there are many ways to meet the challenge.

Chapter 1 presents a perspective and framework for judging the timing and location for advantageous real estate investment in light of our volatile economy.

Chapter 2 covers the characteristics of real estate that set it apart from other types of investments. These traits offer advantages for anyone who is serious about becoming financially secure and willing to make the effort required.

To a large degree, real estate analysis is learning how to use your own good judgment. Chapter 3 covers the easy-to-use methods that apply to any investment to help determine the likely level of risk and profit.

Chapter 4 introduces techniques for measuring the financial performance of real estate investments.

Chapter 5 expands the methods of controlling risk in the context of recurring real estate cycles. Awareness of cycles is an important tool, given the magnitude of ongoing economic swings.

If you are just starting your real estate acquisition program and don't have a lot of cash, you may find Chapter 6 helpful. It contains techniques for acquiring real estate when you don't have cash.

Investing in real estate is most often a process of negotiating and structuring financing. Methods designed to finance real estate are covered in Chapters 7 and 8.

Chapters 9 and 10 present the application of leases and options in real estate acquisition.

Chapter 11 contains techniques you can use to increase value, solve problems, and protect your investment.

Chapter 12 covers many of the ways to apply the nontaxable exchange.

This is a book of practical techniques. These street-wise methods are the result of years of real estate practice by investors and brokers throughout the United States. They are the financial formulas that power the steady rise to security and independence of people from all walks of life, and now they can do the same for you.

Real Estate Acquisition is based on the other books I have written. I have attempted to distill the important themes and expand them within the context of this strange new investment cycle. In an attempt to increase the ease of reading and usefulness for a larger audience, I have avoided overly technical legal and accounting explanations. As with all my writing, I have tried to keep the reader at the front of my mind in the hope that my somewhat different view of real estate and the world will ring true.

Chapter One

Putting Real Estate in Perspective

Although investment real estate is owned and successfully managed by many people who have no formal business education, it is still serious business. Jobs produced by housing construction and real estate-related manufacturing and sales form an essential component of our economy. The employment benefits of new home construction and the resulting sales of appliances, carpets, and furniture filter down through the entire economic system.

When building is booming, the economy is booming. When building slows, it often signals the coming of a recession. Working like a lead anchor, a drop in construction drags down employment and consumer spending and even deflates our sense of national well-being. We never really end a recession until housing construction and sales lead us out of the slump. At least that is what has happened with every recession since WWII.

How Supply and Demand Work for Your Success

The fluctuation of supply relative to demand creates the market in real estate. These two forces continually demonstrate their dominance throughout all aspects of our economy. The investor who doesn't learn how these basic economic forces work is likely to run into trouble. Understanding how the balance shifts between supply and demand at different times in different locations can greatly increase your opportunity for success and help you avoid problems.

Not long ago, thousands of residential and commercial lots were arbitrarily created out of cattle ranches in New Mexico and Arizona, and sold in New York and New Jersey. When many of the investors grew tired of making the payments and tried to cash in, they found there were no buyers. There was a growing supply of lots but no natural demand. In fact, both the supply and the demand had been created by out-of-town promoters. The local Realtors in the Southwest whom the owners contacted in an attempt to take their nonexistent profit had to explain the economic facts of the land market to the hapless investors. Some of these land sales operations are evolving into healthy growing communities, but it has taken a long time. I remember being out of town at a real estate conference when a broker-investor tried to hand me the payment schedule and related paper work for one of these lots, saying: "It's yours. I don't want it." I declined.

Learning the distinction between promotionally generated artificial demand and the natural demand of an established growing community is mandatory for risk-aware real estate investment. You can tell the difference by looking at what is behind the market activity. Is it the natural demand for real estate resulting from solid business and population growth or is it the artificial demand of promotion? One is an opportunity for profit; the other is at best a long wait. The best fundamental indicator for demand is the job market in your investment area. Are jobs being created, holding steady, or is an unemployment trend developing? Answer these questions and you will have a pretty good handle on the potential for real estate demand.

There is an historical case involving one of the first land-sale operations in the west. A promoter bought some grazing land on the northeast edge of town and divided it into one-acre lots. He then ran ads in the larger cities and set up a sales office just outside the local train station. As people arrived by train, he drove them out to the ranch and touted the money they could make with a $100 lot investment. Sales were just not happening. After a year of this frustration the promoter made a small change, and a year later the subdivision was sold out. When the real estate market woke up to inflation in the early 1970s the lots were reselling at $1,000 and by the mid-1970s, they were at $3,500. By the 1990s, they were selling for $100,000 and exclusive custom homes were under construction. How did the original promoter kick start sales after the first year? He bought an old drilling rig from an oil operation, put it in the middle of the ranch, and had it fired up when the prospects from the train station drove by.

In spite of your best efforts to evaluate the market, natural demand compressed into a short time span often attracts unexpected over-speculation. This recurring human tendency produces the greater fool syndrome. Here buyers seem eager to pay more than the property is worth under normal market conditions in the hope that they can sell it at a profit to the next wave of speculators. The problem is obvious for the end buyers. To whom are they going to sell?

One glaring example of this occurred during the last housing cycle top. A wild-eyed, cash-heavy speculator who had just sold property in California moved into town, buying five newly constructed houses on a single block, marking the top of the market and making front page news. How in the world could that be a good idea? It wasn't. What happened to buy low and sell high? It got so heated that some builders refused to sell unless the buyer planned to live in the house. They were concerned that all the empty homes were hurting the market for their subdivisions.

Although many make large profits by getting in and out of an overheated demand market, the ultimate end is the bursting of the bubble. The good thing about the extremes in real estate cycles is change. Prices eventually return to a more rational relationship with supply as demand cools and normal population growth absorbs the excess supply. However, in the credit-dependent real estate market, the return to some semblance of normal balance can take years of debt-ridden agony.

There is a long history of speculative excess in all types of investment markets, from land sales to tulip bulbs. When it gets out of hand in real estate, though, it can be extremely dangerous because of the large amounts of debt and long time period necessary for the market to clear. It's not uncommon for an oversupply of property to be on the market for years.

Real estate market fluctuations cannot be put in proper perspective unless you consider the time factors involved. It may indeed be the case that a community started as a land sales promotion will grow to a city of 100,000 happy residents, but when? Until that day approaches, don't count on demand other than that generated by the sales force, working hard for those commissions. It may be true that there is a housing shortage, but that does not justify an irrational speculative boom based on the hope that prices have no ceiling and the fear that you may be left out.

Value adjustments resulting from shifts in supply and demand can make investment timing crucial. Initial demand has a way of leveling off and going through a period of consolidation before continuing upward movement. Unfortunately, it is common for a large supply of property to come onto the market at about the time demand slows down. Expect builders to make every effort to create the supply requested by demand. After all, they do have an incentive; and unfortunately, that can lead to trouble.

A contraction in a generally growing real estate market can be an excellent entry point. It is possible to pick up property at reasonable prices, if not bargain prices, when builders are overextended on construction loans and burdened by land inventory. This is one point in the cycle that can be an opportunity for investors with cash and credit and a good relationship with banks. The banks have an incentive, and that can lead to opportunity.

Working with banks that have to clear nonperforming loans from their books is a steady business when the cycle turns down. Usually, banks get around to taking action about the time the cycle is bottoming. Furthermore, by then they are often willing to extend credit to anyone who has the ability to take over the liability associated with the property, even writing down the balance as an incentive. And incentives play a large role in real estate.

Real Estate Investment Success is Time Dependent

Timing and location determine value. Questions of when and where are equally important in an acquisition strategy. Investors who don't ask *when* and blindly accept *where* are potential owners of desert lots. It takes time for the natural growth of demand to build real estate wealth. Careful, steady acquisition in a market you understand is much more profitable financially and psychologically than being caught up in the dangers of speculative greed with the risk of a wipeout.

Real estate markets are inevitably defined in terms of location and time. "It is a seller's market in Houston" expresses very simply that there are more buyers than sellers there at that time. Sellers have greater control over the negotiations and price decisions. "There is a buyer's market in Pittsburgh," of course, means the

9

opposite: more people want to sell than buy, and buyers have the upper hand in negotiations. This is the short-hand we use to describe the activity that is a market cycle.

From the perspective of timing, the best time to buy is just when a market is coming out of a prolonged slump. The best time to sell is just when the market is reaching the cycle top. The difficulty, of course, is telling the two apart without the benefit of hindsight. Nevertheless, today's crisis is forming the base from which tomorrow's millions will be earned. Change is the only constant in our free market. Opportunity wouldn't exist without it. Our past (and future) monetary crises and depressions have built the foundation for greater economic strength and have proven to be excellent buying times for long-term real estate acquisition.

Regardless of what happens in the future, the main task is to be aware that some change will occur and that there is a natural tendency for all markets to seek a rational balance between extremes. If you know what's happening, you can learn techniques designed to work in all types of real estate markets that will help meet your personal and financial objectives.

I was having lunch recently with a couple of old friends when Will asked if now was a good time to buy real estate. My answer was yes, as long as the price is right. Ben, who is actively involved in real estate, added that that is always true. And I think that captures the strategy that best governs any acquisition strategy. The next step is making sure the price is right for your objectives.

The opportunity for real estate acquisition is as varied as the location of property. It's all around us. When to buy is much easier to decide than where. Often, we seem to have little choice concerning timing. I know a broker who always says "buy it" if he is asked to give an opinion about a property that is fundamentally sound. Norm says he has never made a mistake advising a purchase when the basic value is there and the debt is manageable, but he learned the hard way. Norm lost some important clients by being too cautious, so now his theory is that the chances are better doing something than doing nothing, provided the property meets your needs and has limited risk. It's hard to argue with that type of reasoning.

When real estate is booming, it seems that now is the last chance to buy because you won't be able to afford the higher prices that are "sure to come". But who really knows what the future holds? Whatever it is, no investment should be made without a limit on risk and an expectation of profit. Making a decision as to "where" you want to acquire real estate can be as easy as walking out your front door. And, with the right negotiation techniques, "when" can be anytime you choose.

Geographic Flexibility Expands Opportunity

Location of the real estate you acquire will, to a large degree, determine the amount of your profit. Your ability to time and negotiate the acquisition is also very important, but nothing compares with choosing the right location for lowering risk and increasing the potential for success.

Location can refer to a building site in New York or the entire Sunbelt. In choosing where to invest, try not to limit yourself. It is your decision and you should give due consideration to your own state, city, neighborhood, and city block, as well as the potential rental house next door.

Unfortunately, the choice of investment location is too often limited by unwillingness to place money out of town. Finding quality investment property is difficult anyway. Try to keep from holding yourself back because of geography. Diversity of location is a major component of real estate opportunity and it should not be viewed as a problem.

You may feel that you can only invest in familiar locations. Starting with the house next door may be a good beginning if it's for sale and has profit potential. You may find the details of management easier when your investment is nearby, but proximity can also be a source of trouble when tenants have easy access to you.

An acquisition strategy limited to familiar surroundings is a logical and relatively comfortable beginning, but it must take a secondary position to the economics of the market. Why pass up a profit because it is out of town? Just build in a factor for time and travel. And using the same reasoning, why buy property just because it is close to you? The point is that the profit potential should drive the acquisition, even though timing and location underlie the fundamentals of your decision.

11

Some of the best buys are overlooked because of distance. It is easy to read the paper each day and check out the ads or do a search online; but it takes some work and extra effort to establish contacts out of town and to stay in touch until a willing seller turns up. A very successful businessman who specializes in ranch acquisition proved the importance of geographic flexibility to me. Frank traveled throughout the Southwest by pickup to manage his diverse holdings. The more he drove, the more he acquired. The travel eventually became so extensive and his holdings so large that he bought a plane to speed up his travel and increase the time he could spend managing his land. He told me that after a couple of years he realized that he was missing the good buys by literally flying over them. He went back to driving his pickup and visiting with his friends along the way, and his opportunities for trading real estate started growing again. The more he traveled and stayed in contact with friends, the more opportunities he found. For this ranch trader, there was no substitute for face-to-face contact.

It is not uncommon that many of the best buys never reach the open market. Consequently, your friends and contacts become very important to your success. A casual mention of someone who's thinking of selling should never be ignored. It may turn out to be your investment project for next year. I remember being told of a 20-unit apartment complex for sale about 80 miles out of town. I had just acquired a 6 and 16 unit in the same area, so it was natural for the rumor to float my way. The trouble was the other property I owned was easy: nothing down and good cash flow. The 20 unit was going to require a bank loan for the down payment. I was able to negotiate it on favorable terms by assigning the rents as security. It didn't hurt that I was an owner in the town and had a good relationship with the banker.

If you are hesitant about looking out of town, consider starting with the one-hour rule: If you can get there in about an hour, it's close enough. Owning apartments an hour's drive or an hour away by air is practically like being in your own back yard. If a serious problem comes up, you can be there in short order. With competent local management, living far away can even be a benefit if you don't get the calls on Saturday night when the sewer backs up. Don't pass up a good buy because of distance, but do consider time. The location may be economically good and the distance may be inconvenient, but when time and travel costs are negotiated into the acquisition terms, the profit may make the distance shrink fast.

The primary decision criteria must be the benefits the property holds for you. Everything else is simply less important. It may be that for you, the distance of a certain property outweighs the benefits of ownership. A simple question to ask is: Will this acquisition improve my life?

The only limit to the distance of an investment acquisition should be your ability to manage it comfortably at a profit. Even then, distance is not necessarily the deciding variable. Just being familiar with a certain city may be all you need. Develop a willingness to go where the best locations are.

I once met an investor from Boston who was on his way to close the purchase of a 40-unit apartment complex in Denver. He already owned 20 units, which he had acquired while living in Denver two years earlier. He was comfortable with owning real estate in Denver, although it was a couple of thousand miles from where he lived. The economics of the property made the distance secondary because Hank had a good understanding of the financials. He had a computer printout on the property, which projected a discounted cash-flow analysis for the next 10 years.

There are probably many opportunities nearby that can be acquired with the right combination of negotiation techniques. If you have time to buy them all, you may find you've made enough money to travel on vacation instead of searching for property. Nevertheless, with growing national affluence, and a more determined investing public, the search and competition for real estate can often be a frustrating process. This places greater responsibility on you to build value into the terms of the acquisition. Negotiation skill and knowing the right combination of techniques play an important role in success. Value is not absolute, nor is it always readily apparent. Ultimately, it is what you do with the property that often makes it worth the price.

Different people see different opportunities at different prices. One Texas investor bought a vacant building that no one in Santa Fe would touch and turned it into one of the most successful small shopping malls in town. Being from out of town, he saw profit possibilities where local investors only saw another run-down building. He actually had seen a similar project in a different state and applied the idea here. His model has since been used with several older buildings around town with great success. I guess one person's hometown is another's out of town. And if you keep that in mind, adapting to distance is just another management task.

Buying in the right location is not quite enough. You must buy at the right time. Your acquisition decisions must fully consider the effect of time on location and their combined effect on your investment return. Market values are not determined in a vacuum. Value is determined by the fundamentals of employment and population growth acting on supply and demand in a specific location during a specific time period. Not all good locations are good at all times. Time provides opportunity. Location provides opportunity. It's up to you to recognize the combination of time and location that will meet your objectives.

Real estate markets and business in general tend to move in cycles. A well-timed acquisition in the business cycle will help. Entry at the wrong point in time can be miserable, if not downright costly. The rule is to buy low and sell high, but how do you know when? One thing that might help is to think in terms of market trends, duration, and direction.

Answers to a few questions can help you determine the right timing. Has growth in this location just started? When did it start? Has this town been through a boom-bust cycle before? When? How long will the growth continue? When might it end? When will the consolidation period occur? Will supply catch up with demand and wash out a few investors or builders? Where do you want to be invested if a slowdown occurs and what level of risk protection do you need to ride out temporary corrections in the supply-demand struggle?

Being aware of the timing possibilities goes a long way toward maximizing your profit and minimizing your risk. Seeing the potential of a down-and-out area may give you financial security faster than many obviously booming markets. There are dangers in a boom and profits in a bust.

Real Estate Can Cost Too Much

Our economy has more than 150 years of rhythmic expansion and contraction. Behind an increase in the number of families, which would seem to indicate greater housing demand, lurks the danger of excessive credit expansion and an inflationary blow-off, ending in a severe economic contraction. Cycle fluctuations have always been with us and probably always will be to some degree. Economic peaks and troughs should not be feared. You can adjust to them and learn to profit. They are helpful timing indicators and form the basis for investment opportunity.

For example, years ago there was a genuine housing shortage. It was the result of the imbalance between supply and demand that grew out of an increase in the house-buying age population. The imbalance and demand-pull force on housing prices then was steady to the point that a myth developed in the model-building financial community that house prices never go down. It is sad that well-documented economic history is ignored in the mathematical models of lenders. Unfortunately, credit was generated based on this misconception and money went in search of borrowers. This easy credit atmosphere was supported by a permissive regulatory policy that combined with the creative securitization of mortgages to unleash a tsunami of credit that swamped the housing market in the early 2000s, leaving a wasteland when it receded. That is how real estate can cost too much. It is also how cycle peaks can form. Incentives can outweigh good judgment when money is involved, even with banks. The financial community was making too much money in the short run to consider the consequences of their negligent underwriting and sometimes fraudulent business practices.

In a normal well-regulated market, borrowers search for lenders and often feel assured that if their loan is approved it is verification of a good purchase decision. Many final real estate decisions are made on a borrower's trust in the analytical judgment of the bank. After all, the bank is filled with financial experts. It's a hard reality to learn that the banks are not in business to protect you or your money. Their purpose is to take care of themselves and they have strong incentives to do so. I can't remember all the times I've heard potential investors say that if the bank will lend me the money, I will do the deal. It's like transferring responsibility to a third party who must know more than you do because they work at a bank. Character, collateral, and capacity to repay the loan are what a bank wants from a borrower, and those are often independent of the merit of the real estate involved.

Real estate investment is the best chance most of us have to own a share of America. If you doubt this, take a moment and look at the immigrant community in your area. Watch them work hard, gradually accumulating a real estate base. Each property they acquire is a rung in their ladder of financial independence.

As our population increases and as more people become aware of the benefits (if not necessity) of owning real estate, chances are that demand for investment property will continue, regardless of credit availability and the ups and downs of the economy, and the folly of excessive debt.

All the strength and prosperity of the country won't prevent an occasional and sometimes predictable economic contraction, a housing bubble and burst, or financial crisis. These slumps will probably prove to be exceptional buying opportunities at a time when most will fear to invest. A rational perspective requires balanced expectations. But when the recessions pass, and growth and prosperity seem too good to end, and everyone is overly optimistic, it is time for caution.

Nothing in the economy is forever. Inflation carries the seeds of deflation. Deflation carries the seeds of inflation. Economic expansion has always been followed by economic contraction. Longer cycles contain these somewhat regular up-and-down patterns and form the history of our national prosperity and well-being. To expect prices to continue rising forever can result in dangerous investment decisions. To expect a depression to continue forever is equally useless. An extreme and rapid price increase is an opportunity to sell at top dollar. A depression is an opportunity to buy at bottom dollar.

The challenge in any investment trend is to learn to participate profitably regardless of the direction. This requires restraint when most people are optimistic and aggressiveness when most are pessimistic. You must own something to sell as the market is topping and you need to conserve your cash and credit to buy as the market bottoms. Of course, there is plenty of opportunity between the extremes. With an awareness of economic fluctuations, you can decrease your risk and increase your likelihood of making a profit.

When you are faced with an irrational market dominated by speculation and there seems to be no property to buy, keep in mind that eventually there will be a change. Although houses and income property are viewed as a hedge against inflation, there is a price at which the public will view real estate as too expensive. Prices will then level off or drop to more reasonable levels. The dream of an investment that produces overnight fortunes has a way of eroding our more reasonable tendencies. But reality catches up when the monthly mortgage payment has to be made and the income to pay it just isn't there.

Nothing illustrates this better than the case of the vacant land owner who suddenly realizes that the monthly payments are competing with payment of normal living expenses. Only then is it discovered that no one seems to want to buy the land at the same tidy profit that had been planned on by the former friend who handled the purchase.

In one sad case, a widower purchased several hundred acres at a price that was above the actual market. His daughter was married to the listing salesman, who needed the commission. One year after the acquisition, things changed. The daughter was divorced. The widower had borrowed against his stock portfolio to secure the down payment loan and the stock market was dropping, forcing the bank to call for more collateral. Although he tried to sell on several occasions, no buyers were found, even at a loss. The private mortgage holder (the original seller) would not return phone calls or consider renegotiating the loan payments. Foreclosure seemed inevitable.

It is especially easy to make a bad buy when things are booming. It is equally difficult to get out when the market turns down. The problem is that in real estate, the process takes years and people have short memories. An investment should be made only on its own merits, not on the blind trust of relatives, friends, or in-laws, or in the hope of finding a bigger fool to sell to later. One of the ironic realities of the investment world is the tendency people have to buy when it's time to sell and sell when it's time to buy.

Real estate is not exempt from the universal laws of price movement and the flow of value between supply and demand. Nor are real estate investors blessed with gifts of vision unknown to investors in different markets. Even in real estate, there is a willingness to buy and sell along with the rest of the crowd. Speculative excesses are just as dangerous in real estate as they are in the stock market, and the consequences can be just as damaging because of the important role of real estate in our economy.

Sell when everyone wants to hold. Buy when everyone else is afraid to, not because prices are necessarily lower than two years ago, but because you have better control of the negotiations and can build in more of a profit, and limit your risk. You can negotiate better terms when the owner does not want the property anymore. Your ability to control the negotiation tends to be limited when the owner thinks he's sitting on a gold mine.

General market conditions don't necessarily make a specific property a bad buy. There is a middle ground where reasonable people can meet and set up a reasonable deal regardless of the state of the economy. When the seller can take or leave the deal, you give up a little in risk protection now and profit down the road.

Even when general market conditions don't provide the advantages you would like, there are techniques to turn the deal in your direction. You can take certain steps to structure any transaction to your advantage, to smooth out the worst possible effects, and to maximize the potential benefits.

You may think a certain property is not for you; the buyer may want too much money up front and the location may seem bad. But before you write off the deal, ask yourself what you can do to change the property and the terms of the offer. As the competition for investment property increases, the necessity for creative negotiation will become more important. Each investment opportunity should be carefully analyzed and negotiated before going to the next. Thorough analysis, skillful negotiation, and realistic expectations are the foundation of successful real estate acquisition.

Understanding the American Dream

The American Dream is to own a home, and with good reason. Pay it off and you have basic financial security. At least you have a place to live if you don't have a job. And living in a free and clear house after retirement has its rewards. The housing speculation we saw in the first half of the 2000s shows how a good idea can be carried too far on top of a credit bubble. It does not have to be that way for you. The baseline of any investment strategy is cash flow stability and home-life security. You need income and a place to live that won't be lost when the next bubble bursts.

Self-reliance and critical thinking are values you are likely to appreciate. I say this because you have read this far and may have a natural affinity for questioning accepted wisdom and doubting the sales pitch that is so common in our popular investment culture. Using cycles is about thinking for yourself and making your own decisions. Look for ways to move against the tide at the right time, neither too early nor too late. Leverage before inflation takes off. Deleverage before deflation takes hold. But at any and every opportunity, strive to pay off your home. Here are a few things to consider.

1. You don't truly own your home if there is a loan on it.

2. If you have extra cash and are paying more interest on your home loan than you can earn in a risk-free investment, you will be ahead by paying off your home and avoiding the interest.

3. Capital preservation is the first rule of investing. A paid-for house follows the rule and is about as risk-free as you can get these days.

4. You will increase your monthly income by the amount of the loan payment.

5. That cash flow can then be invested each month if you like.

6. Don't borrow against your home to buy consumer items. Consumer debt is a burden in this deflationary investment environment, not a form of investment leverage.

7. Cash flow is very important when appreciation is lacking.

8. Net cash flow is what counts. Any loan paid off increases your net income.

9. Personal control over net cash flow is always better than

stock market risk, unless you are unusually skilled and make your own buy and sell decisions.

10. Safety and income beat risk and loan payments every day.

11. If you seek advice about paying off your home, ask someone with no financial interest in your decision. Don't ask a financial advisor whose income depends on keeping your money under management.

12. Financial freedom is escape from a certain level of anxiety.

13. *No debt* is the definition of freedom in today's debt-ridden society.

14. Cash flow extraction is the business model of our service economy. Relentless increases in health insurance, medical care, tuition, cable TV fees, cell phone access, gasoline, food, consumer debt interest, bank fees, property taxes, and car and home insurance are some examples. Try to be on the receiving side of that trade, not the paying side.

15. Are the dividends from the stock you would sell to pay off your home less than your mortgage payment? If so, paying off your house will increase your cash flow.

16. If you have enough cash in the stock market to pay off your home loan and you are considering it, how will you feel if the stocks go down to the point that you don't have enough money to pay off the loan?

17. A free and clear house is an asset you can borrow against when an investment that is too good to pass up comes along. Strange, pay it off so you can borrow again. This is flexibility and source of inexpensive credit.

18. Interest is for getting, not for paying.

19. Buy a home you can afford, then pay it off. Many never make that investment and have nothing to show for a lifetime of paying rent.

20. Paying interest on a home loan is like renting, except you are renting money. Rents tend to increase as inflation erodes the dollar. Adjustable rate mortgages will increase just like rent and for the same reason. Avoid rent, ARMs, and home equity loans.

21. If you buy a house and have a $200,000 30-year loan at 6 percent, you will pay interest of $231,676.38 over the life of the loan. It's like paying twice for the house.

22. The tax deduction for interest is helpful when compared to rent or if it moves you to a lower tax bracket, but that is where it ends. Interest deductions cost real money. Each dollar you pay is a dollar you don't have, despite being able to say that you benefited in a certain amount because you deducted it.

23. Just because a lender approves your large loan doesn't mean it's a good idea. Don't take approval by the lender personally. You are the one who has to pay the money back.

24. If you apply for credit, at some point you will be asked if you own or rent and the amount of your monthly mortgage payment. Saying yes to own and zero to monthly payment is best.

25. Don't build or buy more than you need or can use. The loan is harder to pay off if you get caught in a down cycle, and the amount of anxiety you experience will be in proportion to the debt you are carrying. Down cycles will always follow up cycles.

Chapter Two

The Natural Advantage of Real Estate

Real estate is one of the few investment vehicles that can provide financial security and independence as a result of your own initiative. You don't need a lot of money or a lot of specialized technical knowledge to get started. An average amount of common sense, consistent effort, and a desire to learn will put you far ahead sooner than you thought possible.

This point was illustrated by Ray, who inquired about a group of commercial buildings I had advertised for sale. Although Ray didn't buy the property (a fact he often lamented later), he did reveal his interesting and successful acquisition strategy.

Ray was a draftsman who spent his coffee breaks and lunch hours searching the local newspapers for new real estate ads. His objective was to read the paper every day and get to the good buys before the other guys. Ray was so successful in his real estate search that his supervisor couldn't stand it and looked for any excuse to cause him trouble at work. The supervisor envied Ray's life style because Ray owned a country estate, drove a sports car, invested in land and income property, and actually made more money from his lunch hour searches than from his job.

Finally, the envy and mystery got to his boss, who found a minor excuse and fired him. This was all Ray needed to devote full time to real estate acquisition. His lunch hour real estate projects actually forced job independence on him in less than three years. Consistent effort provided the experience, and in time, real estate freed him from the necessity of working for others. Now Ray works by choice and with considerably greater compensation, acquiring and sometimes selling investment real estate. In fact, when we last spoke, he was a bit surprised because he had just sold some apartments and was suffering depreciation withdrawal. His tax bill had increased.

Four Reasons Why You Have an Advantage with Real Estate

It's the nature of real estate that gives you the edge. And in today's investment climate, we need all the help we can get. Certain characteristics of real estate make it destined to play an increasingly important role in our lives over the years to come. Clearly, it is a subject of great concern when the cycle races to the bottom and the jobs provided by the real estate industry disappear. This occasional process is an inescapable illustration of human folly concentrated in one industry, usually residential housing. When this happens, the central role of real estate in our economy moves to the front as unemployment rises. However, cycles fluctuate, and a crisis often contains opportunity.

There is no sure-thing investment, and every opportunity involving money warrants caution. Nevertheless, each type of investment has a personality that is reflected in its price behavior. You can actually learn about the market behavior of different types of investments by watching their price action. Ultimately, how much money an investment takes out or puts in your pocket is determined by its price fluctuation. Well-chosen real estate tends to be more price-stable than the stock market. But more importantly, real estate has certain characteristics that give you a degree of direct influence over its value.

The objective of investing is to make money. Whether you want money for financial security or to spend on the good life, or both, is up to you. Regardless of your purpose, you may already realize that real estate acquisition is one of the most controllable and practical methods to meet your financial objectives. There are, in fact, four major advantages inherent in the ownership of income real estate.

1. Rental Income. Rental income from improved real estate is one of the few sources of relatively passive income. Cash flow from income property is for the most part produced by the capital asset itself as distinguished from earnings that result from your personal efforts. Consequently, you can set up a situation that, in effect, provides you with a salary, but does not place the demands on your time that a job does. Furthermore, by being able to raise rents as inflation warrants, you have an advantage over many jobs.

Rental income results from ownership, not employment. This is the basis of financial independence and security, whether you are retired or a young entrepreneur.

2. Appreciation. Appreciation is another characteristic that works to your advantage. Normal investment appreciation results from the interaction of supply and demand in the marketplace. There is a long history of a gradual increase in the value of land, which is the foundation of real estate. Of course, the speed of appreciation varies depending on the supply-demand balance in a given location at a given time. And appreciation of real property is sometimes distorted by overheated speculation, inflation, and surprise deflation. But historically, values have increased steadily with population growth as the supply of land decreases relative to demand.

3. Tax Shelter. Tax shelter usually refers to the artificial (not actual) loss, resulting from the depreciation of real property. This can sometimes be a double advantage. Both rents and some other income can be sheltered from tax. As time passes, the law requires depreciation of the value of the property as an operating expense. With certain limitations, if the depreciation exceeds the rental income when combined with other operating expenses, the resulting loss is then deducted from other income, thereby sheltering it from tax.

4. Equity Buildup. Real estate acquisitions are usually structured with financing that covers the majority of the cost. As the loans are paid (often with the rental income produced by the property), equity builds up; the portion of ownership that is free and clear of debt increases. When you consider that the loan is reduced with rent paid by tenants, it's easy to visualize equity buildup as a savings account that increases each month and is available for use when you sell, refinance, or exchange.

All of these benefits can help as inflation forces us into higher tax brackets, while higher living costs erode real purchasing power. Unfortunately, the simplicity of the process has been complicated by changing tax laws. For example, active involvement in management per IRS guidelines is a requirement for full realization of tax benefits.

Another form of tax shelter is the favorable treatment available for long-term capital gain. This lower tax rate is a favored plaything of Congress. It bounces around a lot, so watch for changes through the years.

One of the best friends you can have is a good accountant to keep you up to date on the rules and help you stay out of trouble. Practically, this means having the tax consequences reviewed by your accountant prior to buying or selling with the same care as you would expect when your attorney reviews the contract prior to signing. Both legal and accounting reviews are required due diligence for a serious acquisition strategy. *No surprise* is a core rule.

Rental income, appreciation, tax shelter, and equity buildup are the measurable benefits normally associated with real estate. They each contribute to tangible profit when you eventually establish the total return on income-producing real estate. Each benefit has value that can be measured.

Real Estate Has the Edge

You are more likely to become rich and stay rich by owning real estate. If you have made the decision to accumulate wealth (regardless of the reasons), the probability of success is greatly increased if real estate ownership is part of the plan. If you are already wealthy, the chances of keeping the real value of your estate increase when you own real estate.

If you don't have much to start with, it's a slow process to build an estate by trading stocks. This is true even if you're an expert, simply because of the nature of the stock market. Of course, the ownership of a well-timed purchase of stocks has a place in a balanced investment portfolio, but when you're first starting out, the odds are in your favor with real estate. The advantage over stocks is, in part, due to the leverage available with real estate.

Years ago, I met a young salesman who had about $1,200 left after a prolonged effort at beating the stock market. Joe had just married and decided it was time to get serious about making money. He closed his brokerage account, took the $ 1,200, and made a down payment on a rental house. Over the next four months, he borrowed down payments for a triplex and duplex. Within one year, he had regained all the money lost in the stock market. Soon he quit his job, started wheeling and dealing in real estate, and was financially independent five years later. As he told it: "I finally noticed that the people who made money and kept it owned real estate."

You can verify the relative performance of people who apply concentrated effort in real estate and those who follow the financial markets. Just look at the people you know. How many are more secure in their real estate portfolio than in their stock market efforts? If you want to go a step farther to get a statistical reading on your chances, check the rate of success on bank trusts that invest in the financial markets (but shy away from real estate). It doesn't matter how much money you make from time to time if you can't keep it.

It takes a high degree of specialized skill to succeed in trading financial markets and usually several years of painful losses, not to mention a reasonably large nest egg to practice with. Financial markets have a place, but the wide, difficult-to-predict fluctuations place a heavy burden on even experienced money managers.

In contrast, the unique characteristics of real estate work in your favor. It can be a forgiving investment. If you make a mistake, you can apply a few techniques, adjust the financing, wait for the right time, and sell out to a more appropriate owner, hopefully at a reasonable profit. Your initiative can make a difference if the cycle turns against you. Sweat your way out of the problem if you have to (remodel). There are many ways to apply self-reliance when you own real estate.

One of the interesting aspects of real estate is that at certain times certain property just seems to be right for certain people. A friend of mine actually specializes in acquiring property in a 10-block stretch of one street. It's a run-down industrial area that Bill knows better than anyone in town. As a result, when owners are retiring or need to sell, they approach him first because they know he is not afraid of the area and will be able to meet the terms of any private financing they negotiate. Bill entered real estate after retiring from a successful sales career. He found a niche in real estate that he liked and understood. These large, well-built, old buildings were selling well below replacement cost; often by trust departments in local banks who had cared for them on behalf of widows who wanted income rather than an empty old building.

Bill knew that market; although nervous at times, he was eventually able to lease whatever he bought. When he retired, Bill negotiated ownership of his employer's warehouse as part of his retirement compensation. You just never know what is possible. It's always best to keep an open mind and try to find the right questions to ask.

One day I was talking with Mary, an escrow officer who had skillfully closed many of my larger transactions over the years. She told me of a conversation years earlier with an old timer in the real estate business. How, she asked him, can I make a million dollars? It's simple he said, just buy a rental house a year.

This little story is one of the best statements of a practical real estate acquisition strategy I have ever heard. It grew out of being able to ask the right question. All you need is the consistency to stick with your plan year after year. Management talent helps and can be learned. Keep your regular job and avoid excessive debt. Before you know it, you own something worth having.

It is really not difficult to find properties if you keep in mind that circumstances are constantly changing for every one of us every day. What may appear to be a disaster for one person is the foundation of prosperity for another. The nature of real estate can form a hidden opportunity for your acquisition program. Finding property that someone else doesn't want is the starting point. The more they don't want it, the better your chances of negotiating a favorable acquisition that meets your interests and theirs.

Another aspect of real estate that gives you an edge is its inseparable dependence on credit. You're really not expected to pay cash for real estate. In many cases, you don't even need approved credit. Negotiated leverage is expected and is an indispensable advantage when you know the full range of financing techniques available. Normal down payments can range from virtually nothing on certain government-backed mortgages to 25 percent down on bank-financed commercial projects. And of course, private financing is even more flexible, depending on the parties involved. There are no absolutes when it comes to financing real estate. And the rules (if any) change with the cycle as credit expands and contracts, influencing the liquidity of real estate.

There are no standard requirements for cash outlays in real

estate. Many new projects are totally put together with loans. Developers actually try to mortgage out by limiting their costs to the amount of the construction financing. Occasionally, in privately financed transactions, the purchaser is paid by the seller as an incentive to take property. It often depends on the circumstances of the owner in relation to the supply and demand balance of the market. It is this cyclical nature of real estate that creates opportunity.

These, of course, are extreme examples, but they illustrate the vast range of opportunities available to anyone who knows even a small percentage of the many techniques that can be customized to acquire real estate.

You Have More Control with Real Estate

There is one characteristic of real estate ownership that can work in your favor or against you: control. From beginning to end, from acquisition to sale, you personally are at the helm. It's your thought and action that must determine your decisions and the success of the acquisition. The techniques you use to negotiate low risk and maximum profit in the beginning, the problems of ownership and management, and the final sale decisions maybe years later, all rest on you. It's your thought and your action that control the outcome within the dynamics of the real estate cycle.

Owning investment real estate is similar to owning a small business, but perhaps a little easier. If the real estate market turns against you, time and patience can bring you out on top eventually. If a small business topples, normally you're just out of business (unless you're especially talented and think of a winning idea).

Many years ago, when drive-in movies were coming of age, the father of one of my best friends was struggling to keep his new drive-in open. He could not break even with all the competition in town. Marlin had exhausted his capital and local credit and was driving to Dallas to borrow more money. Half way there, he had an idea and literally turned around in the middle of the road and headed home. His idea led to more drive-ins and ultimately to the sale of the real estate they occupied, which provided the income for his retirement. He made money from the movie operation and retired with the income from the sale of the land bought with the money from his idea. The insight he had was simple and brilliant: charge a dollar a car load for admission and make the profit on popcorn sales. His drive-in filled immediately every night with cars, and the cars were packed with people, and they bought a lot of popcorn and paid for many acres of prime real estate.

Real estate offers any number of problem-solving opportunities. You can divide the property, increase or lower the rents, upgrade the appearance, restructure the financing, and take any number of steps involving personal effort to protect your investment.

This type of concentrated effort is often just icing on the cake. If you acquire real estate at the right time and with a negotiated balance between risk and profit, time and location will do most of the work for you. Your personal effort will contribute to the success, but it's the nature of real estate to provide financial protection normally missing in other types of investments.

Buying at the right time in the right location is the best thing you can do to speed success. A wise decision along these lines is worth more than a little time and effort. One of the most successful and well-respected real estate brokers I had the privilege of working with has a valuable expression that summarizes this idea: Real estate success is being in the right place at the right time. George knew what he was talking about. The fortunate part of this truism is that there are so many right places that by just being around long enough, you're likely to hit some of them. Of course, you have to be able to recognize when you're there, and that's not always easy.

Money, success, wealth, security, or whatever your objective is, can only be found (or lost) on specific real estate deals. Just getting into real estate is not the answer; it's the first step. You must get into the right property at the right time in the right location and then you can go to work. After establishing your positions, coincidence may work to your favor. Certainly, chance is on your side with real estate. We live in a world of economic swings. Real estate ownership can be a way to profit from and to smooth out these extremes. It's a path open to all, without exclusion.

Why Real Estate Ownership is a Necessity for Most of Us

Generally speaking, there are three reasons to start an investment program: to live comfortably now, to have the funds to live comfortably later, and to leave an estate. Financial security is the best summary of these three reasons to invest. Although there are always opportunities, the frustrating effects of inflation, stagnant incomes, and the greed-fueled folly of our financial leaders all increase the challenge. Even in this context, a growing population is combining with concern over inflation to create a steady growth in demand for investment real estate. Real estate remains one of the few independent roads to financial security that anyone can use to offset inflation and a stagnant income.

The realization of the important role of real estate can come at the strangest times. One of my real estate friends was weaving his way through an IRS audit when he got on this subject with the agent, a single woman two years from retirement. Innocently, the agent started complaining about continual rent increases and how she wouldn't be able to make do after retirement. It was a reminder of one reason you should plan to own a house free of debt when you retire.

There is a type of push-pull relationship between inflation and taxation that involves anyone who earns money or has an income and pays taxes. The more you earn, the higher the percentage of your income that goes to taxes. Our progressive tax system was originally intended by Congress to minimize taxes at lower income levels so basic needs could be met and to maximize taxes at higher levels where primary needs were not a concern. The problem today is that basic needs cost more, yet the progressive income tax structure permits you to retain an increasingly smaller percentage of each additional dollar of income, thus reducing needed income at the mid level. Although you may earn more each year, the combined effect of higher taxes and reduced purchasing power due to inflation may actually lower your standard of living. It's what you keep after taxes and inflation that makes you wealthy, not what you make.

It is generally thought that doctors are wealthy people. I accepted this generalization until I met one who had recently been divorced. He was making high monthly alimony payments and was committed to monthly child support payments. He was paying rent on an apartment (no deduction), supporting a car, and owned no real estate. A high before-tax income put him in very serious financial trouble, and he was borrowing to pay income taxes. Inflation, a nondeductible life style, and a high tax bracket took away money intended for basic needs and forced him into debt. Paying the interest on his growing debt was like throwing money out of a moving car at eighty miles an hour. In the eyes of the IRS, he was a single, high-income, high-tax bracket wage earner, but he was literally going broke. It took some thoughtful real estate acquisition and debt restructuring to reverse the trend.

How to Measure Your Investment Return after Taxes and Inflation

To measure the net return of any investment, you must account for the reduction in purchasing power due to inflation and the payment of taxes related to the investment. Inflation and taxes must be treated as expense items to arrive at a net return, which is your real investment return. This is what you have left in purchasing power. The bench mark is the point in time when you make the initial investment. The objective is to measure the net money you receive from a specific investment in a certain time period. To do this accurately, you must determine what was earned after subtracting taxes and inflation. This is your real aftertax return. It's this net return that counts.

The Consumer Price Index, commonly referred to as the CPI, is the usual source for our news reports on inflation and it's the basis for increases in Social Security payments. There are other indicators you can use to track inflation. For example, the Personal Consumption Expenditures (PCE) core rate is preferred by the Federal Reserve (Fed) to set monetary policy because it doesn't fluctuate as much as the CPI and the components are more to the Fed's liking. Statistics are everywhere, but what matters is the price increase of the items you must have to live. Simple awareness is all you need to see what is happening.

The *nominal* return is what you usually see quoted for most financial instruments. The *real* return is what is left after adjusting for inflation. However, it is best to also consider the effect of taxes

31

and calculate a *real aftertax return.* For our purposes, we will use a one-year time period. First, subtract the tax from your investment income; then, deduct the inflation that occurred during the year. The remainder is the real aftertax return (or loss). Note that the inflation dollar amount is calculated based on the capital invested and the interest income.

Example: Jack receives 5 percent interest on a $1,000 corporate bond. His effective tax rate is 30 percent, and the inflation rate is 3 percent. Jack's real aftertax return is 0.35 percent, not 5 percent. With this type of debt investment, Jack is fighting just to stay even, as his capital and interest income shrink by the rate of inflation.

Calculation:
Interest: $50 (0.05 x 1,000 = 50)
Less tax: $15 (0.30 x 50 = 15)
Equals: $35
Less Inflation on invested capital: $30 (0.03 x 1,000 = 30)
Less inflation on interest income: $1.50 (0.03 x 50 = 1.50)
Equals: real aftertax return: $3.50 (35-31.50 = 3.50)
Real aftertax rate of return: 0.35% (3.50 / 1,000 = .0035)

Apply this same analysis to a savings account that pays one percent on a $1,000 deposit and you can readily see the damage done to savings when our economy is in a low interest rate cycle and inflation is holding at 3 percent. The real return becomes negative, which means purchasing power is lost every year.

Integrate awareness of taxes and inflation into the way you view the investment world and it could change your approach to all types of investing. The importance and popularity of IRA and 401K plans become easy to understand. Consider taxes and inflation in your investment thinking and you may be able to overcome a couple of the biggest investment barriers we all face. Keep in mind that the *nominal* return and the *real* return are different, as is *aftertax real return.*

Investing is an attempt to transfer purchasing power through time while protecting it from inflation and deflation. If you accomplish this basic purpose, at some time in the future, your investment will be there for you in real purchasing power to provide the financial security and standard of living you want. And if you can shelter it from annual taxes, it will grow faster and result in a larger end amount.

Vary the numbers and figure the actual effect of taxes and inflation on your investments. Try a higher inflation rate. The steps are the same. In fact, you can determine the current percentages for taxes and inflation and calculate your real net income, whether from investments or salary. Awareness of the effect of taxes and inflation on your investments is the first step toward changing the situation.

Real Estate is a Hedge against an Unknowable Future

The four major benefits of real estate, each in their own way, help protect you from financial surprises:

1. Rental income helps if you lose your job or are retired.
2. Appreciation is a buffer against inflation.
3. Tax shelter offsets the cost of government.
4. Equity buildup acts as savings.

All work together to increase the probability of a financially successful investment. Simply stated, real estate is a good business with a low barrier to entry. Its unique benefits provide more access to financial security than you may have thought possible. The relatively unrestricted opportunity for personal initiative provides opportunities as well as risks, but the risks are really no different from those of other investments. The rewards are often much greater and, in most cases, far outweigh the measurable risks.

Today's volatile economy has upended traditional investment markets. Yield is hard to find in the stock and bond markets with any sense of safety. During a recent dinner party, I was talking with a retired business executive who had decided to balance his portfolio by expanding his investment in rental houses. Ken had concerns that the risk-adjusted return of the stock and bond market was out of kilter. After about a half hour of market talk, he told me that he was accelerating the loan payoff on one of his rentals because the income from rent was high relative to his debt service.

He was close to having it paid and asked me if I thought that was a good idea. I said I did, because I always favor paying off debt when possible. I told Ken he was close to having income that was safer than any bond he could buy at today's prices. This is smart planning by a retired executive who knows what he's doing.

Income produced by property is just one of the components of total value. Land appreciation is another plus. Depreciation and the resulting tax savings can also be viewed as a value benefit. Each factor must be evaluated separately, then combined to arrive at a decision about the appropriateness of a specific property for you. Often this process requires a decision concerning risks in relation to the potential for profit. First, protect yourself by negotiating terms that offset the maximum potential loss—for example, a loan with no personal liability. Second, consider the greatest gain and negotiate the transaction with terms designed to achieve it. When you have explored the extremes and planned for them, you've set the stage for reasonable expectations, which is all anyone can realistically anticipate.

Chapter Three

How to Minimize Risk and Maximize Profit

There is really only one question that should govern the decision to make a particular real estate investment: What is the probability of earning a certain profit in a given time period?

All the details of analysis and market research work toward answering this question. Of course, there are many other less quantifiable and more emotional reasons for deciding to acquire certain property. One investor said his mother didn't trust buildings that weren't made out of brick, and since she was lending him the down payment, he couldn't look at apartments that weren't brick. Or, sometimes we have personal reasons of identity associated with the property we choose. Pride of ownership probably plays a bigger role in real estate than easy credit. For example, consider the following statement, "I'm not interested in that type of property and no one that I would be associated with is, either." In this case, it did not matter that the return was 25 percent and that there was full occupancy; it was on the wrong side of the tracks.

Sometimes it is not monetary reward or financial risk that has the last word. Too often emotions outweigh financial gain, and the outcome is a purchase at the top of the market and a ticket for a ride to the bottom. It is this emotional factor that should be considered prior to any investment commitment. Certainly, you must buy what you want, but people who buy for emotional reasons often end up in trouble. Putting the personal aspects aside, there is only the relationship between profit and loss that governs the financial benefits of real estate investment. However, what we choose to invest in cannot be separated from our self image and identity. Both are important to happiness.

During the question period following a speech on the real estate market, a very concerned woman asked me how anyone could buy apartments when there seemed to be so many under construction and advertised in the paper for rent. My answer reiterated the importance of the relation between supply and demand. A seemingly large supply doesn't necessarily mean high risk when the demand is there. The new supply of apartments was being steadily absorbed by an expanding population. Housing needs were growing in leaps and bounds, rents had increased to a profitable level in spite of high interest rates, and developers were trying to catch up with demand. And as the new units came on line, ads were placed in the paper as part of the rent-up phase. Certainly, there were more units, but there were more renters too. Supply and demand were both growing, but demand was growing faster, and the supply wasn't likely to catch up for a couple of years at the current absorption rate.

Common Sense Investment Analysis

At the crest of the recent housing cycle, a local investor did what might be the best maneuver to minimize risk. I heard this story during a discussion of the importance of paying off loans on personal residences. This investor acquired 40 rental houses over a period of several hard-working years. He had grown tired of the management but hadn't anticipated the topping of the market. It was just lucky timing. What was this risk reduction maneuver? He sold 20 of the rentals and paid off the loans on the other 20. Debt-free cash flow and a 50 percent reduction in management burden just as the market is topping is one good decision for minimizing risk.

Risk comes in many forms. There is market risk. This is, for example, a reduction in demand due to a loss of jobs in the area, resulting in a population exodus and increase in apartment vacancies. There is credit risk. This is the chance that financing may not be available when a loan is due on a commercial center. There is interest rate risk, which is the chance that rates will increase to the point that borrowing costs are not supported by the cash flow of the property. There is competitive risk—for example, a new area of development that draws tenants from existing buildings. Each of these risks damages the cash flow of a property and jeopardizes continued ownership. The consequences of this damage are reduced or eliminated when property is owned free and clear.

We can further refine our pursuit of minimum risk and maximum profit with two common sense questions, which you can answer at the level of detail you prefer.

1. Will the future cash flows exceed the expenses by a satisfactory amount? It is difficult to forecast the future, but an attempt to project past performance into a range of expectations is basic to all business, including real estate.

Lay out the property's past performance and project it into the future. The key to accuracy is completeness. Compare pretax and aftertax income. Take a close look at vacancy rates and all expenses, maintenance and capital improvements. It is important to consider the net proceeds when you sell. The cash you receive when you sell is as much a part of cash flow as monthly operating profit: It just happens to come in a lump sum later on. If you want to go even further in your analysis, discount all the net cash flows by the anticipated rate of inflation to determine your real return on investment (inflation-adjusted purchasing power).

2. What are the chances that you're wrong, and what do you do if you are? It makes good sense to have contingency plans. Protection can often be negotiated into the acquisition terms, such as no personal liability and partial release clauses in the case of vacant land. Although the sky's the limit, there is nothing like a safe exit for a good night's sleep. Plan for maximum profit, but negotiate risk protection into the deal in case circumstances you can't possibly foresee shoot down your projections. What do you do if a major employer leaves the area and vacancies increase? Can you lower the rent to attract tenants and still meet the loan payment?

The most likely outcome will prove to be on the middle ground somewhere between optimistic dreams and worst fears. Mapping out the possibilities in advance and even quantifying their effect on the rate of return can go a long way toward ensuring that a plan actually happens. You may even discover that the suspected dangers have little or no effect on the project's overall rate of return.

Learning to quantify concerns is a big step toward common sense. If you hesitate to take action because of an anticipated problem, try to reduce the issue to a range of costs, then plug the figures into the projections and see if the effect on your rate of return will be significant. Learning to combine common sense with cool mathematical analysis will separate you from unsuccessful emotional buyers. You may see potential overlooked by the seller as well as by other investors. It may just turn out to be your insight and hard work that make an income out of what others see as high risk and potential loss. The one thing that can hold you back is failure to rely on your own common sense and good judgment.

Avoid the High Down Payment-Low Risk Trap

The possibility of financial loss is not eliminated by making a large down payment. Profit is not necessarily assured either. Although most people associate a large equity with safety, the reality of the matter is that the more money you commit, the more you have to lose if things go against you.

Making a large profit with little risk of loss is the product of knowledge and good judgment, not money. I know one investor who had an effective strategy that served his acquisition program well. Over a period of approximately eight years, he acquired property valued at more than $10 million. He began with no money but he was a whiz at math and a skilled negotiator.

His technique was effective and simple. It was a combination of negotiation, analysis ability, and good management. It began with a purchase agreement that was contingent on refinancing the property in an amount large enough to pay the existing loans and to meet the down payment requirements of the seller. In many cases, this included funds to remodel the complex. The negotiation key involved convincing the seller to carry a portion of his equity on a second mortgage.

Paul would offer to purchase a complex, such as the American West Apartments, with a $475,000 down payment, provided he could arrange a new first mortgage. As part of the offer, the seller would be asked to carry a second mortgage for the difference between the purchase price and the new first mortgage. Often, he was able to negotiate the price down and the property appraisal and new loan up. This reduced the amount of the second mortgage. He would occasionally divert part of the new loan proceeds to do major repairs on the apartments, which pleased the seller. Even though it increased the second mortgage it added quality to the property and confidence in his managerial ability. The down payment came from the new first mortgage.

> *Example*: American West Apartments
> *Original Terms*
> Price: $1,300,000
> Less existing loan: 500,000
> Equals equity: 800,000
>
> *Acquisition Structure*
> Price: $1,300,000
> Less new loan: 975,000
> Less second mortgage: 325,000
> Equals equity: -0-

There is a mathematical requirement that must be met for this technique to work. The existing mortgage must be lower than the loan value by an amount large enough to pay it off and satisfy the seller's need for cash. This means that the appraisal of the property, for purposes of the new loan, must be high enough to generate the cash necessary to pay off the existing loan and still leave at least enough for a down payment satisfactory to the seller. Therefore:

The old loan ($500,000) and the down payment ($475,000) equal the new loan ($975,000).

The sales price ($1,300,000) is the sum of the new loan ($975,000) and the second mortgage ($325,000).

The seller's equity ($800,000) is the total of the down payment ($475,000) and the second mortgage ($325,000).

Paul always included a clause in the purchase contract that required all costs of closing to be taken from the new loan proceeds and that any costs he owed were to be added to the second mortgage. He acquired property without any money of his own. In fact, he often pulled cash out as a result of proration and appraisals based on remodeled value that were higher than his purchase price. The seller got the cash he wanted and avoided the liability of a new first mortgage. When Paul pulled out cash, he pledged to the seller to use it for remodeling to satisfy the appraised value.

Lenders often look favorably on projects that a developer can put together with skill alone. One mortgage broker put it this way: "Lenders respect a developer who can put a project together without any of his own money. It shows that he knows what he's doing." One banker told me he liked working with a particular developer because he always did financial projections that reflected reality and removed a concern from the bank.

How to Avoid Losing Property

Income property is best when it stands on its own merits, not on the financial statement of the investor. This operating principle is fundamental to avoiding the "greater fool" trap of irrational speculation. The success of a real estate investment is not guaranteed by a large down payment, nor is it necessarily endangered by a small down payment. The net income-producing ability of the property now and in the future is the best measure of its financial strength, and this is often assured by means other than a large cash outlay. For example, the trend and momentum of the market cycle are primary. A 50 percent down payment still leaves 50 percent debt to be serviced. If a severe rental vacancy occurs, you have a problem that isn't solved by the large down payment.

It may take a large down payment or it may take none at all to gain control of a certain property. Negotiated terms of the acquisition will decide the degree to which you are in control and will establish the assumptions for the initial financial projections. Then your management ability will be called upon to keep costs down and income steady, and to determine whether your initial plan can become a reality. The amount of down payment is often a function of the seller's emotions rather than financial requirements of the project. This emotional aspect can be a benefit for you because of the opening it provides for negotiation.

If the property you're trying to acquire gives off signals that indicate future foreclosure, then something may be wrong with the deal. It could be a problem with the property, such as location, or a problem not necessarily concerning the property itself, or even traffic flow. It might be a problem with the loan terms or it could be poor management. If you are worried about losing the property you acquire, the less down payment and personal liability the better. Consider the economics of the property, the financing, and your own management ability to ensure that foreclosure is a distant and remote possibility. Unfortunately, there are operators who try to structure impossible financing, then sell to poor managers in the hopes of foreclosing later and reselling. If you run into one of these characters and discover his intentions before it's too late, get out fast. It is much better to find sellers who don't want property back.

In any event, work toward structuring investments so you can't get seriously hurt no matter what happens to the property or the general economy. Value in real estate is ultimately determined by what you can do with it. By careful negotiation and analysis, you can protect yourself against loss by never extending a commitment beyond the limits of what you and the property can sustain.

The Important Role of Negotiation

Negotiation skill can, in effect, replace money, but money can never take the place of a good negotiator. Fortunately, negotiation skill can be developed. You can learn to work with people. And you can learn to move the course of events in a mutually beneficial direction. Sometimes gaining the upper hand is difficult, and in certain situations there's just no way to reach a mutually beneficial compromise. There are people who will not give an inch on their terms. It's this type of tough, seemingly unreasonable negotiator who can teach us a few practical lessons.

Strength in negotiation is built on giving the impression that you don't need success. It may be that you want the negotiations to succeed very much. But you gain the upper hand when it is apparent that you can quite easily walk away from the deal without the least amount of pain. And you can train yourself to walk away from a deal when the terms are not right and you can't seem to make them right.

Even though you may have to leave a few opportunities on the table, never close the door. Walk away with this attitude: "Maybe we can talk about it later." Be interested without being needy. Develop patience. Accomplishing a worthwhile acquisition can take a long time. Develop confidence. If you miss an opportunity, keep in mind that you will eventually find another. Negotiation is not necessarily an exercise in giving up terms you want. It can be a creative process of discovering alternatives, not thought of previously, which may make the deal better than originally planned.

When you are faced with the necessity of backing down on a point, it is often better to talk around it and to get the entire transaction set up before you give in. When you do give in, do it suddenly, and accept the whole deal. Structure your compromise so it cements all aspects of the negotiation. In other words, try to work in the points you want (every one of them) as a condition of accepting the compromise.

Never give the impression that you're willing to give in just for the sake of making the deal. Present what works best for you as poker-faced as you can. If it is not accepted, keep pulling out alternatives until you find a combination that works. Keep negotiating in a collected and unemotional manner either until the deal fits together or you run out of alternative proposals. If it works, fine. If it doesn't work, neither give up nor give in: just say goodbye and look for other property. You may even get a phone call offering a solution that is better than you would have ever asked for. There is always another chance, and there always will be.

Strength in negotiation comes as much from your attitude toward yourself as it does from your attitude toward the seller. Have confidence and believe that if a certain deal falls through, you'll just go on to the next one, until you succeed.

The Mechanics of Buying

There are four general processes characteristic of most real estate transactions:
1. Negotiating the terms (often in writing);
2. Agreeing, in writing, to what you negotiated (signing);
3. Arranging any loans necessary; and
4. Closing the transaction.

Each step has certain routine requirements, which are designed to complete a deal smoothly. Although it can be a source of comfort that much of the paperwork is handled by specialists (brokers, lawyers, escrow agents), it does not relieve you as the buyer from the responsibility of understanding what is happening every step of the way. It is your money, your property, and your responsibility to maintain control and to avoid becoming an inadvertent victim of circumstances, or worse.

The initial negotiation process is your first opportunity to gain some degree of control and to set up the transaction the way you want it. This is when the various acquisition techniques come into play. The terms reached at this point may very well determine your profit when you sell. It is the most important stage in any acquisition. From this point on, it gets increasingly difficult to make changes.

Negotiation is your chance to include the techniques that will limit risk and maximize profit. Ask and you might get. All they can say is no. The point is that real estate acquisition starts with bargaining, known in polite circles as negotiating. No one is going to give you what you want unless you ask for it, and now is the time to ask.

Asking requires two things:

1. Willingness to lay your position on the line during the talking stage when a meeting of the minds is in the process of forming; and

2. Close attention to detail to make sure that what is agreed upon during oral negotiation makes it to the written agreement.

It's very important to get a written agreement as soon as possible. Gains made during initial negotiations mean nothing if they don't end up in the written agreement. Expect nothing until you have it in writing. It's easy for misunderstanding to develop when you're talking about somewhat complex acquisition terms. Even when you have the terms clearly defined in a purchase agreement, problems can come up later. It is important to make sure that the terms of the original negotiation are actually included in the final documents. Even the best lawyers can leave out important points that may have a direct impact on your future income.

In one transaction, an unintentional error in an important document almost reduced my cash flow by $600 per month. The purchase agreement stated that the monthly payments on the second real estate contract would increase to $1,000 per month, "including interest," after the existing first mortgage was paid in full. When the final contract was typed the sentence read "$1,000 per month *plus* interest." Fortunately, the sellers willingly made the necessary change when I caught the error during closing. If it had gone through undetected, in six years, the escrow agent would have routinely presented a very unwelcome surprise. It would have been very difficult to correct after all the documents had been recorded and the people involved had gone their various ways.

You have to track the progress of what you agree to during negotiations and make sure the documents are worded correctly. It helps to let as many eyes review for errors as possible; one more person with a fresh viewpoint may catch something previously overlooked. The purpose is not to catch someone making a mistake, but to help each other work through the transaction with as few errors as possible. When the going gets complicated, the more solution-oriented helpers you have the better.

When you get past the written agreements, you essentially have a deal. What follows is simply a routine process of carrying out the agreements. Believe it or not, there are many transactions that go through closing without a hitch. It is normal to have problems in business, and if you have trouble dealing with them normally, consider whether you really want to set up a program of real estate acquisition. It's the calm, cool, and collected who take home the profits year after year. If you are a person who gets upset easily, plan on being unnerved regularly when you enter the real estate market.

Although you may have done some preliminary investigation, the next step involves going through the details of setting up any loans necessary for completing the acquisition. This is the one aspect of any real estate purchase that must go routinely, for a very good reason: institutional financing should be virtually assured before you sign the purchase agreement. If you have to go through the process of obtaining financing, say so in the purchase agreement and make the transaction contingent on financing. But keep in mind that until all contingencies are met and removed from the agreement by signed acknowledgment, you don't have a transaction.

You have an edge if you make the basic arrangements for an institutional loan before you get into the details of negotiation. You have to know how much money you have before you can negotiate from a position of strength. Whether the money is from your pocket or from a bank's vault is of no concern to the seller. You must know that you can close the deal you agree to before you start talking.

It's a different story when you are arranging for the seller to carry back a portion of his equity on a purchase money mortgage. Instead of the bank holding the mortgage, the seller does. This financing technique provides one of the best opportunities for negotiation and problem solving in real estate. You don't have to fight the policies of a lender and you have a chance to give and take a little with the seller, who also has an interest in seeing the deal go through. Closing should follow naturally from the written agreements. When working with an established escrow or title company or attorneys, you can usually rest assured that they will do the most professional job they're capable of. If you are not closing with an established escrow company or attorney, be prepared to encounter a few problems. In any event, never consider the deal final until closing has been completed and you are the owner of record.

Why the Nontaxable Exchange Is Important

The exchange of real estate under the provisions of Section 1031 of the Internal Revenue Code is one of the few real tax shelters left. It is the technique that allows any real estate held for investment or business use to be traded for other investment or business real estate without paying capital gains tax.

This is important because completing an exchange preserves appreciation and maintains compounding of equity through continued ownership. Exchanging has probably helped more people build wealth than any method available today. It is the ultimate technique for maximizing profit in real estate.

The law is clear and there is a safe harbor that ensures protection against challenge by the IRS. As long as you legally avoid actual or constructive receipt of the cash or non real estate property (boot) involved, the transaction can be, depending on the details, tax free. If you get or have the legal right to money or boot (constructive receipt) involved in the exchange, the realized gain on the property will be recognized in that amount. You can have a partially taxable exchange under Section 1031.

The reality of the market developed this technique, which has been legislated by Congress and explained by IRC Section 1031 regulations. It solves the problem of how to find property and exchange with an owner whose property you want, who just happens to want your property. The law provides a structure that permits you to find a buyer, transfer ownership, and hold the money in trust with a third party under an agreement that prevents constructive receipt of the proceeds, which means the exchange contract must limit your legal right to the cash used to purchase replacement property. The contract must conform to the regulations, and all parties must follow the terms of the contract. No shortcuts.

Within 45 days from transfer, you must identify the replacement property. Within the earlier of 180 days from transfer or the due date of your tax return, including extensions for the tax year of the transfer, you must receive ownership of the replacement property. This safe harbor rule does not mean you can't still do a simple exchange with an owner that does not involve a sale of one of the properties. It just outlines a framework for a deferred exchange that ensures nontaxable treatment of the transaction when a third party is buying one of the properties. It is designed to protect you against constructive receipt or legal right to the money used to acquire replacement property. This protection is provided by the rights and obligations established by the documents, which must be followed to avoid tax.

Exchanging is very important when the gain is large, capital gains rates are high, and you plan to acquire other real estate. Why sell, pay tax, and buy property with the money left? It is a much better strategy to exchange. For details, see IRS publication 544.

Chapter Four

Methods for Evaluating Real Estate

Investment analysis can be a simple, direct, and useful process when your personal objectives are clear. We analyze to clarify choice. The choice is usually between alternative investment opportunities. But with real estate, we don't have an array of properties to choose from. Consequently, the choice is often limited to whether the property will meet certain investment objectives.

The generally accepted method of analyzing all investments is to determine the annual rate of return (percentage) expected on the capital committed to the venture. Normally, the rate of return is expected to increase as risk increases. Consequently, when you compare investments, you are faced with the challenge of deciding acceptable trade-offs between return, risk, and the general unknowns of the future. The return on real estate is the result of the fundamentals that act on it: population and job growth, site location, traffic flow rental appeal, highway access, all affecting the rate of absorption of land, commercial and residential rentals.

When we look at financial performance resulting from fundamentals, we focus on cash flows compared to money invested, which is also a cash flow. It helps to keep two factors in mind: total cash flow generated by the investment and the resulting percentage rate of return on invested capital. When you have a fairly satisfactory idea of these two figures (even if they are estimates), you can determine whether the potential warrants investment or continuation of the search. Analyzing an investment is a process of comparing the dollars you get out with the dollars you put in over a certain time period. It's this relationship that produces the rate of return. This rate, or percentage return, is compensation for putting capital at risk, foregoing liquidity and, in some cases, allowing others to use it for a limited period of time. The following example illustrates the rate of return, or cash on cash return after expenses and debt service, on a new rental house purchased with a $10,000 down payment.

Example: Cash on Cash Return

Price: $160,000
Less loan: $150,000
Equals equity: $10,000

Income: $15,000
Less vacancy and expenses: $4,000
Equals net operating income (NOI): $11,000
Less debt service: (30y, 5% fixed): $9,663
Equals net annual income: $1,337

Cash on Cash Return: 13.37% (1,337 / 10,000)

In this example, the cash on cash return is calculated based on the money invested as down payment. It's an application of the universal rate of return investment gauge. The percentage return is simply the relation between money invested and money received over the year. If the house were purchased with all cash and no debt, the return would be lower and so would the risk of loss.

Example: All cash purchase

11,000 / 160,000 = 6.875% (NOI / Price = Annual Rate of Return)

Comparing these two acquisition structures shows the importance of leverage and provides a clue to its popularity. Often, using leverage prudently is the only way to increase the return. It's natural to real estate and central to its benefits. The four benefits are easy to remember if you recognize that the first letter of each combine to spell RATE: Rental income; appreciation; tax shelter; equity buildup. All have the potential to produce cash at different times during ownership. Rental income is usually received monthly. Appreciation is realized when you refinance or sell. Tax shelter shows each year when you pay income taxes. Equity buildup is converted to cash at refinance or sale. Each benefit has a different source and comes at a different time, subject to variations in the economic cycle.

When money goes into a savings account or certificate of deposit, the bank lends it out at a higher rate for profit and uses the loan-asset to leverage its capital and increase overall investment activity. Interest is, in a sense, rent paid by the bank for use of money. At points in the cycle, the return on this type of deposit can be next to nothing and hardly seem worth the trouble. Over the years, I have seen CD investments at 12 percent and at 1 percent, depending on the state of the economy and the credit cycle.

If you put $1,000 in the stock market you, must analyze a different set of variables to determine the return on investment. Here, there is a choice of stocks that may pay dividends and hold the potential for appreciation or loss. Therefore, to accurately measure the rate of return, you must consider the contribution of dividend payments (if any) and the appreciation of the stock (if any). If the dividend on a $1,000 stock investment is $40 and the stock increases by $100 in value to $1,100 during one year, what is your pretax rate of return before commissions? ($40 dividend plus $100 increase in value = 140 / 1,000 = 14%).

Of course, taxes, selling expenses, and inflation reduce actual purchasing power if you cash in the investment at the end of the year. Since aftertax returns vary with different individual tax brackets, the common practice of thinking in pretax rates of return is an accepted way to compare investment alternatives, or so goes the argument. But it's really not that difficult to adjust the return for the taxes. In fact, it's essential in a real estate investment because of the tax benefits. And it's not much more of a problem to plug in a factor for inflation and its reduction in the purchasing power of the money you receive. When you know the procedure, you can make these calculations using the adjustments appropriate for your situation. And if nothing else, awareness of taxes and inflation and deflation form a good backdrop for thinking about the merits of any financial strategy.

Rate of return is a percentage expression of the dollar yield produced by invested capital, usually during one year. Calculations are made on an annual basis either to compare trends of years past or to project possible performance in future years. The basic concept is the same for determining the performance of money placed in a savings account, the stock market, or real estate. When you establish a rate of return, you state the relationship between three variables: your initial investment, the income it produces, and the time required to produce the income.

The capitalization rate (Cap Rate) in real estate is a common adaptation of this procedure. It is calculated by dividing the net operating income (NOI) of a property by the price to establish a percentage. (NOI is scheduled income less vacancy and expenses before debt service.) This is the annual rate of return of a debt-free property. You can also determine the value by dividing the NOI by the average Cap Rate of similar properties in a given market area. By doing this calculation, you capitalize the income to arrive at a price, which allows comparison of different properties using a percentage. You can then see if the price of a property is out of line with the value of similar properties, based on income. It is simple and can be very helpful.

Example: Cap Rate = NOI / Price
Say you own six apartments that throw off cash of $24,000 (NOI) after expenses but before depreciation and debt service and you think the complex is worth $600,000. What is the Cap Rate?
24,000 / 600,000 = 0.04

Example: Price = NOI / Cap Rate
The Cap Rate can also be used to set the price when you know the Cap Rate of similar properties in the area. Value is determined by dividing the NOI by the prevailing Cap Rate:
24,000 / 0.04 = 600,000

Notice that the Cap Rate is always calculated as if the property were free of debt and before depreciation. The Cap Rate is sometimes referred to as the overall rate (OAR) when the percentage figure is based on the average of the prevailing Cap Rates of comparable sales in a specific market. The OAR establishes a value derived from an average range of closed sales, allowing comparison across different markets and comparison of different types of income property. Other methods of determining likely market value include comparing recent sales or the replacement costs of similar property, both based on square footage. These two additional valuation techniques can be useful, but ultimately it is the income of an investment that counts most.

What if you discover that the OAR in this market for similar property is 6 percent and you want to determine the price that represents? All you need to do is divide the NOI by the OAR (overall (cap) rate) to get value assigned by the market. In this case, the OAR is the average Cap Rate of properties in the market:

Example:
24,000 / 0.06 = $400,000

As you can see, increasing the Cap Rate produces a lower value. This means that investors who have cash and are willing to buy real estate are likely to require a larger 6 percent return than the 4 percent return offered. When expectations are high for appreciation, lower Cap Rates are more likely to be accepted. When a stagnant market is dominant, and appreciation is difficult to visualize, higher Cap Rates become the norm. Income and cash are in high demand when the cyclical tendency is toward deflation and deleveraging. When inflation cycles into the economy, it is best to be in assets that tend to appreciate.

Measuring Cash Flows over Time

Fortunate timing and a macro-grasp of the real estate market reduce the need for analysis, but that combination is rare. However, I remember renting an apartment when I was in college in the early 1960s from Gary and Carol. They lived in a large older house in an elegant neighborhood a short walk from the university. As Carol gave me the key, I noticed an array of many keys in the cabinet. Through the years, I learned that this economics professor and his wife had bought rentals all over town and especially around the university at early 1960s prices. They eventually turned over management to an established realty company and went on with their lives. These purchases were before the inflation of the 1970s and the increase in the price of oil and real estate. What fortunate timing they had. They bought heavily years before inflation hit public awareness. It must have had something to do with understanding economics.

We separate the benefits of real estate and define them in terms of their essential components: dollars invested, dollars received, and time. Financial analysis is a process of isolating these three factors and determining their relationship in the context of economic cycles. It can be a process of simplification, putting variables in a structure that is useful when making a decision to buy, hold, or sell.

By considering the role of time, you have an opportunity to significantly improve your perspective. In certain business ventures, it is possible to reinvest the cash flows internally for expansion. This concept is not unlike the internal compounding of annual appreciation, characteristic of real estate in general and land in particular.

I remember discussing compounding with an investor-friend many years ago when the issue of the time required to double an investment came up. I explained that an investment that compounded monthly at 7 percent would double in 10 years. This rule of thumb went on to frame much of his investment thinking through the years. The simple calculation behind this guideline can be expanded. When you divide 70 by the number expressing the interest rate, you get the number of years it takes for an investment that compounds monthly to double: (70 / 7 = 10 years) (70 / 14 = 5 years) (70 / 1= 70 years). Little things like this can change the way you view the exponential growth central to investment.

Math Note: Mathematicians will recognize this as an adaptation to monthly compounding based on the continuous compounding of the natural log of 2: $\ln(2) = 0.693147181$ that is related to the yearly compounding rule of 72 used by accountants. All reflect the doubling time of different compounding periods: 69 / 7 = 9.86 years for continuous compounding; 70 / 7 = 10 years for monthly compounding; 72 / 7 = 10.29 years for annual compounding. These are rules of thumb and are not meant to reflect precision, especially at higher values. However, the concept of exponential growth is very important to understanding the numbers of everyday life.

It is the same process for the equity appreciation of a land investment and for a debt investment of a loan. For example, paying 14 percent interest only on a loan means the lender will double her investment in five years if the funds are reinvested and compound monthly at the same rate. You can easily see the trap of a high interest loan for the borrower and why it is often difficult to pay off a high interest loan. Think credit cards.

I remember meeting a math professor when I first started in real estate. He bought a townhouse in a project where I worked and was excited to tell me about his simple technique for paying off his home loan. With amortization schedule in hand he explained: "Each month, I will pay an additional amount equal to the amount scheduled to apply to the principal of the loan, which will cut the term in half. It's a 30-year loan but I will have it paid in 15 years." This works because in the early years of a 30-year loan, most of the monthly payment goes to interest, so the additional amount you pay is very small. As the loan is paid down, the amount of interest paid is reduced and the portion going to principal increases. Every dollar you pay early will remove a dollar from the interest calculation for the next payment and from the life of the loan.

These days that seems like a bit of bother, but the principle involved is important and can be practically applied by paying an additional lump sum to loan principal at some point during the year: The larger the amount, the less interest you will pay over the life of the loan; and the sooner you pay it, the shorter the term of the loan. You get maximum effect by paying an additional lump sum at the beginning of the loan term when the first monthly payment is made. This means that if you pay $500 to reduce the principal when you make your first payment, that is $500 you won't have to pay interest on over the 30-year term of the loan.

An important distinction to remember is that there are two types of investments for purposes of real estate: equity and debt. A lender makes a *debt* investment when advancing the funds secured by real estate. A buyer makes an *equity* investment when acquiring real estate. The buyer gets a deed as proof of ownership. The lender gets a note as evidence of the promise to pay, which is secured by a mortgage recorded as a claim against the property, which can be exercised on default of the note terms. There are other types of debt instruments but this describes the general process.

If you want to trace the future benefits of a venture, you must account for the effect of time on your initial investment and the cash flow it produces. This is when a full understanding of compounding comes in handy. There's really no easy, safe alternative to paying careful attention to your investment capital. If it's sitting in a losing portfolio, it's just a matter of time before you have little or nothing left, no matter which market cycle is in force. The best way to keep a handle on your money is to watch the cash flows in the context of the market cycle. For example, equity investments tend to do best in an inflationary cycle or in a market where appreciation is the trend. Debt investments are preferred in deflationary cycles or in stagnant markets when income is in demand. Both have their time and place.

The purpose of investment analysis is to determine which investment is most profitable and best fits the way you want to live. Are you energized by the challenge of managing your own property and the security of the long-range benefits of appreciation and equity buildup? Or do you prefer liquidity and the freedom from management hassle? Maybe professional management can solve one of your concerns. Maybe the ability to borrow against property can solve the liquidity issue. No matter what happens, you always want to own some real estate.

The following appendix is for readers interested in the time value of money and the details of financial analysis. You may prefer to come back to it later or skip it altogether. In any case, more important issues wait in the chapters that follow, so feel free to skip ahead.

Appendix to Chapter 4: Applying Discounted Cash Flow Analysis

In real estate, we often have the challenge of knowing the cash flows, but not the rate of return they represent when placed in the context of time. This is where discounting enters the calculation. Discounting is the inverse of compounding. When we compound, we determine the cash flows as a result of investing at a given rate of growth per time period. When we discount, we determine the rate of growth per time period represented by known cash flows. In this sense, compounding moves forward in time to determine a dollar amount; and, discounting moves from the future back in time to the present when the projected cash flows are given but the interest rate is unknown. Compounding tells us the dollar amount when the percentage rate is known, and discounting tells us the percentage rate when the dollar amount is known.

The advantage of compounding is easy to see when you focus on the doubling of the dollar amount and how it varies depending on the rate of return:

Example:
Investment ($10,000) Rate 7%
Year 10: $20,097
Year 20: $40,387
Year 30: $81,165

Keep in mind that money invested is always treated as negative because it is money you give rather than receive. Imagine how paying tax in this example would interrupt the compounding growth trend. It's easy to see the advantage of appreciating real estate that grows without ordinary income tax and is taxed at lower capital gains rates when you sell. It's the uninterrupted compounding that produces high and consistent growth. And that is why exchanging tax-free can often be the best choice.

All the calculations that follow were done on an HP 10 B II. For clarity and future reference, each example will be followed by the calculator key sequence. Note that shift indicates the orange key is hit first before entering a number and the orange key command.

Here are the key sequences for the example above, illustrating the doubling at 7 percent with monthly compounding. Notice the minus sign for the money invested or paid out (-10,000).

First, we set the calculator to monthly compounding by hitting 12 shift *p/yr*. If we want annual compounding, we hit 1 shift *p/yr* or for 4 shift *p/yr* for quarterly.

Compounding (Double)
Key sequence HP 10 B II
shift 12 *p/yr*
Year 10: 120 N; 7 I/YR; -10,000 PV; FV = 20,097
Year 20: 240 N; FV = 40,387
Year 30: 360 N; FV = 81,165

Measuring the Benefits of Appreciation and Equity Buildup

Example: Beverly bought a rental house for $95,000 with a $10,000 down payment and a loan of $85,000 and exchanged it 10 years later based on a value of $135,000. Her equity buildup was $13,867, which is the difference between the original loan and the balance at transfer (85,000 - 71,133 = 13,867). Her appreciation was $40,000, which is the difference between the exchange price and the original purchase price. (135,000 - 95,000 = 40,000), both of which we add to the $10,000 down payment to determine the exchange equity (13,867 + 40,000 + 10,000 = 63,867); or more simply stated:

Property value: $135,000
Less loan balance: $71,133 (30y fixed 6% after 120 payments)
Equals equity: $63,867

Key sequence HP 10 B II
Loan payment: 12 *p/yr* 360 N; 6 I/YR; 85,000 PV; PMT = -509.62
Loan balance after 10 years (120 payments): 120 N; FV = 71,133

We count appreciation and equity buildup as separate benefits to focus on the natural advantage of investment real estate. But both combine to form equity, which is determined by subtracting debt from property value.

In this example, the initial investment of $10,000 grew by an annually compounded rate of 20.3726 percent as a result of appreciation and equity buildup. We arrived at this percentage by discounting the equity of $63,867 to $10,000, which means that if we compounded $10,000 at an annual rate of 20.3726 percent over 10 years, we would get $63,867. Here, we solved for the compounded rate of growth by discounting the single cash flow.

Discounting
Key sequence HP 10 B II

56

1 *p/yr*; 10 N; 10,000 +/- PV; 63,867 FV; I/YR = 20.3726%

Notice that *p/yr* is lower case and italics, indicating the use of the orange shift key, which changed the default monthly compounding to annual compounding or, in this application, annual discounting. When you see lower case italics in the following key sequences, it refers to the orange shift key. Also, we changed the $10,000 investment to a negative using the +/- key before entering the amount with the present value (PV) key.

Meaning: $10,000 compounded over 10 years at 20.3726 percent equals a *future value* of $63,867. And $63,867 received 10 years from now when discounted at 20.3726 percent equals a *present value* of $10,000.

Had Beverly decided to sell instead of exchange, it would be necessary to consider the possible tax consequences of the transaction.

Example: Beverly depreciated the property, resulting in an adjusted basis of $60,450, which is subtracted from the sales price to determine the capital gain.

Calculation:
Sales Price: $135,000
Less adjusted basis: $60,450
Equals realized gain: $74,550
Times tax rate of 15%
Equals capital gains tax of $11,183

Without an exchange, the tax paid would reduce the proceeds of the sale and therefore the amount left for reinvestment. As capital gain taxes increase, the available money for reinvestment would decrease.

Calculation:
Equity: $63,867
Less tax: $11,183
Equals aftertax proceeds: $52,684

By completing a nontaxable exchange, Beverly preserves $11,183 in purchasing power that remains in her control for future appreciation in different property.

So far, we have defined the dollar value of the appreciation ($40,000) and equity buildup ($13,867) resulting from Beverly's investment ($10,000). We have also calculated the rate of return represented by those two benefits (20.3726%). Now we will move on to the calculation of the tax shelter benefit and rental income.

Calculating the Tax Shelter Benefits of Depreciation, Expenses, and Interest

Tax shelter covers more than depreciation of property allowed by the tax laws in effect during ownership. It also refers to the loss the property produces, which is deducted on your tax return when depreciation is combined with annual operating expenses and loan interest. Loan principal is not deductible and is the source of the equity buildup benefit. First, we will isolate the dollar value of the depreciation.

Example: We can attribute a dollar value to depreciation by multiplying Beverly's effective tax rate of 28 percent times the depreciation (0.28 x 34,550 = 9,674). This means that Beverly received a tax benefit from depreciation of $9,674 over the 10-year investment. Each year the depreciation deduction was $3,455, which means a $967 cash benefit each year in cash saved from tax (0.28 x 3,455 = 967).

Calculation:
Original cost: $95,000
Less adjusted basis: $60,450
Equals depreciation: $34,550
Times effective tax rate of 0.28
Equals Tax benefit: $9,674

Example: Beverly's loan payment was $509.62 per month and her expenses averaged $250 per month, for a total of $759.62. Expenses include property taxes and maintenance. The tenants paid water, gas, and electricity. The house was practically new

58

when she bought, so no capital replacement costs hit during her 10-year ownership. Vacancy was not a problem due to the high rental demand in the neighborhood

The house was leased during the first three years for $850 per month, and then went to a month-to-month basis for $900 per month for years four and five, then to $950 for the sixth year, where it stayed until she exchanged.

Calculation: The following is a year-by-year list of the net rental income after expenses and debt service. Expenses and debt service total $760 per month, which is subtracted from the monthly rent for that year and multiplied by 12 to get the yearly total.

Net Rental Income:
Year 1: 1,080 (850 - 760 = 90 x 12 = 1,080)
Year 2: 1,080
Year 3: 1,080
Year 4: 1,680 (900 - 760 = 140 x 12 = 1,680)
Year 5: 1,680
Year 6: 2,280 (950 - 760 = 190 x 12 = 2,280)
Year 7: 2,280
Year 8: 2,280
Year 9: 2,280
Year 10: 2,280
10 year total: $18,000

Now we have a picture of the investment benefits of this rental during the 10-year ownership and we can summarize the dollar value represented by each:

Rental income: $18,000
Appreciation: $40,000
Tax shelter from depreciation: $9,674
Equity buildup: $13,867

The actual tax return will require reporting the operating expenses and interest as deductions along with depreciation. From a practical standpoint it is always best to choose investments that make money from operations without regard to tax losses. Calculating the four benefits and their dollar value is to show the many sides of real estate that can work in your favor.

But to see the complete picture, we must deal with the loss that is reported each year on Beverly's tax return and convert it to a cash flow. With that, we will have isolated the entire cash flow stream, including the aftertax income.

We know the expenses for each year but we don't know the interest portion of the loan payment. To determine the yearly interest payment for each year of ownership, we will amortize the loan as follows.

Amortization
Key sequence HP 10 II B
Set calculator to end mode (end does not show in display): shift *beg/end*

Solve for the monthly payment: 12 shift *p/r*; 360 N; 85,000 PV; 6 I/R; 0 FV; PMT

Answer: 509.6179 rounded to 509.62

Don't clear and we will start the amortization sequence as follows:

shift *amort*: 1-12 displays for payments 1-12; now hit the = key

= 1,043.81; this is the amount of principal paid through 12 payments; hit = again

= 5,071.61; this is the amount of interest paid through 12 payments; hit = again

= 83,956.19; this is the balance of the loan after 12 payments.

Now for year two: shift *amort*: 13-24 displays for payments 13-24

= 1,108.19 principal paid during year two;
= 5,007.23 interest paid during year two;
= 82,848.00 loan balance at end of year two.

Using this procedure, here are the interest payments for years 3-10:

Y3 4,939; Y4 4,866; Y5 4,789; Y6 4,707; Y7 4,621; Y8 4,528; Y9 4,431; Y10 4,327

Now we have the year-by-year interest payments, which can be deducted on Beverly's tax return. Next we will subtract from rental income expenses of $3,000 per year ($250 per month),

60

depreciation of $3,455 per year, and the yearly interest. This will tell us the tax loss generated by the rental each year.

Calculation:
Y1: Income 10,200 less (interest 5,072, expenses 3,000, depreciation 3,455) = (1,327)
Y2: Inc 10,200 less (int 5,007, exp 3,000, dep 3,455) = (1,262)
Y3: Inc 10,200 less (int 4,939, exp 3,000, dep 3,455) = (1,194)
Y4: Inc 10,800 less (int 4,866, exp 3,000, dep 3,455) = (521)
Y5: Inc 10,800 less (int 4,789 exp 3,000, dep 3,455) = (444)
Y6: Inc 11,400 less (int 4,707 exp 3,000, dep 3,455) = 238
Y7: Inc 11,400 less (int 4,621 exp 3,000, dep 3,455) = 324
Y8: Inc 11,400 less (int 4,528 exp 3,000, dep 3,455) = 417
Y9: Inc 11,400 less (int 4,431 exp 3,000, dep 3,455) = 514
Y10: Inc 11,400 less (int 4,327 exp 3,000, dep 3,455) = 618

The losses in the first five years of ownership have a cash flow value. We determine that value by multiplying each loss by the effective tax rate. The profits in the last five years are taxable, and to determine their net aftertax value, we reduce them by the effective tax rate paid. In this example, we are using 28 percent to determine the aftertax value of the cash flow stream. The effective tax rate is the tax paid divided by gross income.

Calculation:
Y1: 372 (0.28 x 1,327 = 371.56)
Y2: 353 (0.28 x 1,262 = 353.36)
Y3: 334 (0.28 x 1,194 = 334.32)
Y4: 146 (0.28 x 521 = 145.88)
Y5: 124 (0.28 x 444 = 124.32)
Y6: 171 (0.28 x 238 = 67) 238 - 67 = 171
Y7: 233 (0.28 x 324 = 91) 324 - 91 = 233
Y8: 300 (0.28 x 417 = 117) 417 - 117 = 300
Y9: 370 (0.28 x 514 = 144) 514 - 144 = 370
Y10: 445 (0.28 x 618 = 173) 618 - 173 = 445

This cash flow stream is the aftertax income from rental operations. The first five years represents cash saved in taxes from an operating loss. The second five years represents the cash remaining after paying tax on the profit.

It's a fact of investment life that taxes must be considered. The tax law concerning real estate loss deduction contains certain rules and restrictions relating to active and passive losses and participation in management. Phase out of deductible losses as other income increases further complicates investment real estate. This is again a reason you should always use an accountant. These rules are explained in IRS Publication 925.

Keep in mind that this process started with a $10,000 investment that was leveraged into cash flows from four different sources because of the natural characteristics of real estate. Typically, monthly income is the primary focus of rental property investment, but the other three income sources work quietly below the surface. And they can be effective investment outcomes when converted to cash or exchanged.

Applying the Internal Rate of Return (IRR)

The internal rate of return (IRR) is a method of discounting cash flows to determine the rate of return generated by a property or business project. It can be used to solve for the rate of return when the cash flows are known and realized and it can be used when the cash flows are estimated and projected. It is used to see what an investment returned after the fact and to compare different properties and help make an investment decision. We can apply the IRR methodology to Beverly's investment to determine the rate of return from all sources of cash flow.

Example: The following is a list of the cash flows Beverly realized over the 10 years she owned the house, beginning with the $10,000 down payment, which is a negative cash flow. For simplicity, the calculation is limited to pretax dollars.

Calculation:
Year 0: (10,000)
Year 1: 1,080
Year 2: 1,080
Year 3: 1,080
Year 4: 1,680

Year 5: 1,680
Year 6: 2,280
Year 7: 2,280
Year 8: 2,280
Year 9: 2,280
Year 10: 66,147 (2,280 + 63,867 realized equity)
IRR: 28.3836%

Internal Rate of Return (IRR)
Key sequence HP10 B II
1 shift *p/yr* (10,000) +/- CFj
1,080 CFj 1,080 CFj 1,080 CFj
1,680 CFj 1,680 CFj
2,280 CFj 2,280 CFj 2,280 CFj 2,280 Cfj
66,147 CFj
shift *irr/yr* (answer: 28.3836%)

There is nothing magical about the IRR. It is just the annual compounded rate of return of an investment. It is the same calculation as the yield to maturity (YTM) formula for bonds used on handheld financial calculators. In fact the YTM is the IRR of a bond. The formula for IRR is nonlinear so the computation changes with each cash flow and may develop inaccuracy and multiple answers when there is extreme complexity and excessive negative cash flow. That makes it inappropriate in certain applications. But it works when the cash flows are relatively even, mostly positive, and there is no probability simulation. Keep in mind that IRR is nothing more than a way to discount multiple cash flows to determine the rate of return that is internal to the investment. It is a simple concept, though some try to complicate it. And the best way to keep it simple is to understand how IRR and NPV are related.

Using Net Present Value

Net present value (NPV) solves for a dollar amount. IRR solves for a percentage return. NPV is linear. Each cash flow is discounted separately, and the calculation does not impact the other cash flows. It is basic cash flow discounting and an inherent component of the IRR formula. NPV allows you to set the rate of return you want and then determines whether the investment you are analyzing will return that rate.

Example: The following cash flow projections are the most likely outcomes based on rental history and market trends for this rental property. We are going to solve for NPV the old way so you can see how the process works, using the discount rate factors (present value of 1) for the specific time period of each cash flow at a 12 percent discount rate. After we have the discounted amounts, we will add them to the initial investment to see if the present value of the projected cash flows is greater than the down payment. If the discounted sum is larger, it means the property is a buy because it meets the minimum return threshold. If it is a negative number, it is not a buy because it will return less than the present value of the down payment when compounded at 12 percent. We are asking if the property has at least a 12 percent internal rate of return (IRR).

Calculation:
Year 0: (100,000) down payment
Year 1: 9,000 x 0.892857 = 8,035.71
Year 2: 12,000 x 0.797194 = 9,566.33
Year 3: (3,000) x 0.711780 = (2,135.34)
Year 4: 8,000 x 0.635518 = 5,084.14
Year 5: 150,000 x 0.567426 = 85,113.90

Total discounted amounts: 105,664.74
Down payment: (100,000)
NPV: 5,664.74

This is a positive NPV, which means the projected cash flows produce at least a 12 percent compounded growth of the initial $100,000 investment. In other words, the internal rate of return of the property is greater than 12 percent.

We can check our work using the HP 10 B II financial calculator, which shows an NPV of $5,664.87. One of the many useful things about this calculator is that we can hit the IRR key and see that the actual return is 13.41 percent, which gives us a clue to the relationship between NPV and IRR: The IRR of any investment is the discount rate at which the NPV is zero. In this example, if we discount the cash flows at 13.41 percent, we will get an NPV of zero, meaning that the discounted cash flows equal the $100,000 down payment. The discounted value is neither above nor below the amount invested. It is the same.

Net Present Value (NPV)
Key sequence HP 10 B II
1 shift *p/yr*
12 I/YR
(100,000) +/- CFj
9,000 CFj
12,000 CFj
(3,000) +/- CFj
8,000 CFj
150,000 CFj
shift *npv* (answer: 5,664.8731)
shift *irr/yr* (answer: 13.4095%)

Real estate financial analysis is the process of looking at the inner workings of an investment. When we isolate the contributions to cash flow by the four benefits, we gain insight into the performance of a specific property. It is a step in decision-making. No one would want to make a decision to buy, sell, or hold under conditions of ignorance. Remove the mystery and see what matters in actual day-to-day performance.

During different cycles, different benefits of real estate gain importance. Appreciation during inflationary cycles is of primary importance. Cash flow from rental income is primary during deflationary periods. Free and clear rentals are the best when the economy is stagnant and the clouds of deflation hang over the economy. Highly leveraged appreciating real estate that outruns the depreciation of the dollar is best when inflation is dominant. Money has a time value. However, the utility of money changes with fluctuations of economic cycles and the new risks that keep showing up.

Chapter Five

How to Use Economic Cycles in an Acquisition Strategy

Real estate is a cyclical industry. It expands and contracts with the fluctuations of the supply-demand forces that permeate our economy. Driven by credit and favorable tax treatment, housing often leads the economy into and out of contractions and expansions. We have a 150-year history of market adjustments like this. We thought we knew how to deal with them. Lately, things have changed.

The Great Continuing Contraction of 2008 would be rejected as a fiction novel because no one would believe it. Those who warned of this coming credit collapse were either ignored or attacked as nonbelievers. A few decades of think tank propaganda structured a political system bent on deregulating the banking industry, which blended with a Federal Reserve (Fed) that thought low interest rates should stay low and go lower, resulting in the disintegration of the normal interest rate market and a desperate search for yield by wealthy institutions. As an added bonus, the panicky Chairman of the Fed believed, as only a true believer can, that the banks and financial industry needed no oversight. This is like denying that money is a magnet for thieves.

Enter the bankers, who had turned into financial engineers, with some new ideas to meet the need for yield and earn large fees, with assistance from the rating agencies. Add compliant appraisers and money-hungry mortgage brokers operating with a total breakdown of loan underwriting standards, and the makings of a bubble were in place. The only thing remaining was a public willing to take on more debt, which was easy to find. That is the setting for the real estate market in the early 2000s.

As a result, securitization of mortgages rose like a house of cards, offering high yields for hot money and incentives for the clever to sell to the vulnerable. Mortgage brokers went looking for borrowers so they could create loans for banks to package and sell to the unsuspecting, earning fees unimagined before deregulation allowed commercial banking and investment sales to coexist. Banks, traditionally perceived as fiduciaries, suddenly were incentivized to become self-dealing predators. It has taken time for the public to catch on to the new relationship.

Rating agencies provided the stamp of safety needed by prudent large investors, and the race for yield was off and running. To a large extent, this race was caused by low government bond rates, which were considered safe, but no longer had a high enough yield to meet the actuarial needs of pension funds, life insurance companies, and foundations. This opened the door for new financial products that promised safety and relatively high yield and new riches for all involved. Now the boom-bust structure so common in the history of banking and real estate was complete.

Risk is the ultimate regulator. But if the government stands ready to bail out the banks and cover their losses while letting them keep the profits, where is the risk? Furthermore, when federal regulations are not enforced, there is no way to prevent abuse by the greedy. Lack of accountability is often a precursor to human folly. True, the market will eventually provide discipline. The question is who will be hurt before the market brings down the hammer? Who will pay when the fraud is exposed and who will walk away unchallenged with the ill-gotten gains? How much will the rich and powerful loot from the national treasury with bailouts before the citizens catch on? This is the national treasury. And the money that pays for folly is money that could be used for education, health, and infrastructure. You know, the greater good that seems lost in today's world of special interest conflicts. And worse, when government steps in to protect stock and bond holders with cash, the market discipline of capitalism is lost. And that could bring the whole financial edifice down.

So, we have the princes of finance: the Fed, the banks, and the rating agencies leading the charge up the sand-hill of lax underwriting and irresponsible credit expansion, followed by a trusting public, which for decades had been conditioned to rely on the superior wisdom of these guardians of our national wealth and free market ideology. After all, they have the wealth; they must know what they are doing. *Caveat emptor* is just a couple of Latin words and a distant memory. Such a tease these mortgage brokers are with their adjustable rate loans, selling debt to the uneducated, cash-hungry consumers trying to maintain a lifestyle by borrowing to make up for the death of living wages.

To a large degree, the peddlers of debt to the vulnerable made it as easy as possible to get into trouble. Loans presented at a low interest rate held programmed increases tied to time rather than increases in the market rate of interest. Loan payment increases beyond incomes led the subprime borrowers back down the credit hill to the hell of foreclosure. Jobs tied to the housing market evaporated and a second wave of loss hit the former middle class when there was no income to pay the new loan payments.

Although this was, in part, caused by new financial products, it does not mean there are no legitimate purposes for engineered financial instruments. The mortgage-backed securities market has become essential to the financing of all types of real estate. It holds great promise for the future. This is all the more reason to establish a fully transparent and open market for newly developed security instruments. An open public exchange with full price and fee disclosure might be a good start. Transparency is the key element of a free market and the foundation of the rule of law. Deregulation that hides transactions is reminiscent of the aftermath of the fall of communism and has no place in an honest, fraud-avoiding capitalist society.

In a way, much of what happened is like the difference between gambling and hedging. When you hedge using a properly designed and appropriate vehicle you transfer the risk of legitimate business activity to speculators and investors. When you gamble you create risk that would not have otherwise existed. In hedging an investor, speculator, or trader enters the market knowing the risk and the underlying business transaction. For example, a farmer hedges by selling his wheat to a speculator in the futures market to lock in a profit.

However, when hedge funds and banks buy and sell instruments without a business interest in them and without knowing the quality of the cash flow stream that supports them, both have created a risk that did not exist before. Their actions expose them to new risks and they are gambling, maybe without realizing it. Their reach for profit carries hidden risks and is a gamble for all taxpayers who pay the bills for bailouts. It is also why we still face the systemic risk that continues to build within the banking system. The structure for the next financial crisis is forming a mountain of liability estimated to be so far into the trillions of dollars that to say the amount would encourage disbelief. *The Great Continuing Contraction of 2008* has some exciting chapters to come.

Easy Money Comes to Main Street

In the meantime, as we exit the high-rises of finance on Wall Street, we find that money in search of borrowers has come to Main Street. This is new to local real estate markets. Normally, borrowers had to prove themselves to get loans, but not during this credit bubble. As the 2007 cycle in housing started peaking in 2005 and 2006, it was raining dollars. Flipping houses became the subject of a new TV reality show. Irritating ads for mortgage companies just wouldn't leave the TV in peace. This is how cycle tops are easy to see. Everything associated with housing was just too popular. I remember being at a wedding party in the early 2000s when someone I barely knew, without even saying hello, asked me what I could sell my house for now. I told him I didn't know or care since I had no plans to sell it. There's a clue to what's on the mind of the public.

The tax advantage of deductible interest and tax-free profit up to $500,000 combined with nonexistent underwriting standards and adjustable rate mortgages (ARM) with low initial teaser rates to provide the air for the housing bubble of the early 2000s. Further, home equity loans and refinancing became a way to extract equity from houses in an attempt to maintain a higher standard of living, given the lack of wage increases and predominance of low-paying jobs that started in the 1990s. This was not a good income foundation to deal with the ARM resets that started in the mid 2000s.

In addition, much of our national employment was tied to housing construction. Think about appliances and furniture, carpets, counter tops, and cabinets, and you can visualize the interdependency. When the bubble burst, jobs disappeared, and with them, the income to deal with the debt and cash flow demands of the new housing loans and ARM resets.

Speculation seems to be in our blood. There's a readiness to jump on the latest train to easy money. This time, it was the credit-dependent housing market that issued the siren call to take on debt and buy another house. Circumstances surrounding the credit collapse of 2008 have no modern parallel. Extremes in credit availability and housing speculation were world-wide, but it started here and the aftermath is not a normal business cycle recession. This rancid soup of greed, fraud, and political manipulation has many ingredients and many cooks stirring the pot. As is often the case, it started with changes in the law.

The Role of Law in Real Estate Cycles

If nothing else, cycles expose the surprise of our economic leaders when they finally grasp the presence of the consequences they had long denied as a possibility. Strange how our economy falls into chaos with no idea as to what is happening while it's happening. These accidents reflect an instability that seems resident in our system. Short-term incentives seem to govern instead of considered policy, whether in government or banking.

Underlying the fluctuations in supply and demand that form the normal business cycle are the laws that ensure fair treatment for all citizens. The laws that provide oversight and prevent abuse of the financial incentives that power the economy are fundamental to stability of the system. We need them because, as the late former head of the RTC said, there are a lot of bad people out there. He would know, after cleaning up the savings and loan industry blunder and plunder. However, there is no reason as strong as belief. And when ideology runs amok, sea change becomes unstoppable. Just as they provide stability, laws can introduce instability. And sometimes they lay a clear path to fraud and government corruption. This is unlikely to change without reversal of the legalized corruption of campaign financing and the undue influence of lobbying by the rich and powerful.

Over the last three decades, changes in the law seem to have built a base for financial turmoil and the resurgence of panic cycles that were a long forgotten part of our early history. Deregulation of

70

banking started in 1980. A short review of a few relevant laws will give you the picture. This is further evidence of the truth of Mark Twain's comment that no one is safe while Congress is in session.

The Depository Institutions Deregulation and Monetary Control Act of 1980 combined with *Garn-St. Germain Depository Institutions Act of 1982* to establish the opportunity for the Savings and Loan debacle of the late 1980s and early 1990s. Congress thought it would help the S&Ls earn a profit by allowing them to form investment subsidiaries. The S&L plan for profit was to feed insured deposits into real estate development, causing a boom in office space and all manner of land speculation. The habitual government bailout was followed by the Resolution Trust Corporation selling off property at fire-sale prices. Fraud was discovered, and some participants were prosecuted and jailed. Fraud is a classic companion of bubbles, following easy money on the way up and usually exposed when the top of the cycle is in place. This resolution process took years in the late 1980s and early 1990s.

To contribute to the problem, Congress passed the *Tax Reform Act of 1986*, which limited the tax benefits of passive investments in real estate, among other restrictive provisions. It came just in time to accelerate the demise of the S&L industry, as investment real estate was sold, leaving the S&Ls holding investment positions as the real estate market fell.

After providing all the help the S&L industry could stand, Congress moved on to see what it could do to help the banking industry thrive. Remember, we are deregulating so the free market can grow without government interference. Congress was well supported in its efforts by concerned special interest groups (lobbyists). (For more on the S&L scandal, see *The Big Fix* by James Ring Adams.)

Next was passage of the *Interstate Banking and Branching Efficiency Act of 1994*, which allowed interstate mergers between banks. The stage was set for mergers into mega banks and the familiar too-big-to-fail bailout dilemma. Meanwhile, around this time, a new financial instrument called the Credit Default Swap (CDS) was under design in London—this would play such a big role in the next decade as a clever insurance policy many jumped for and few understood. Of course, they were designed by a bank.

71

New products mean new fees.

The *Taxpayer Relief Act of 1997* reduced capital gain taxes and exempted home sales from any tax on gain of $250,000 for individuals and $500,000 for married couples. This is not exactly a law deregulating banks, but it is a factor in the housing speculation of the 10 years that followed its passage. Why not live in a house for two years while you fix it up and then sell it for a tax-free gain? It makes sense.

Next, Congress decided that banks were different than in the 1930s and a particularly pesky law restricting their activity was no longer necessary (provisions of the Banking Act of 1933 referred to as the Glass Steagall Act). Banks now knew how to behave in the best interests of all the people and were perfectly capable of self-regulation without endangering the public interest. Wishful thinking again, but really, free markets know how to govern themselves. Or so goes the prevailing economic ideology. Besides, the Fed had already allowed many of the provisions to be circumvented.

So, Congress passed the *Gramm-Leach-Bliley Act*, (also known as the *Financial Services Modernization Act of 1999*), allowing the subsidiaries of bank holding companies to expand from commercial banking into investment banking. This change in the law permitted banks to trade for their own accounts and enter the securities brokerage business. In a sense, they were trading with deposits insured by the government. We saw this before in the early 1980s when the S&Ls entered real estate development. Short memories and a blind eye to history are prerequisites for a political career.

Next, Congress passed the *Commodity Futures Modernization Act of 2000*. This particular work of genius removed over-the-counter derivatives from regulation, allowing credit default swaps to crawl down the hole of nondisclosure. As a result, banks could do almost anything they wanted without government interference, while hidden from public view.

For our purposes, it is enough to acknowledge that during the last 30 years, laws were changed to deregulate banking and trading of securities and their derivatives. Further, the laws that remained were ignored or not enforced in the name of free market self-regulation. Now we deal with the aftermath. But is it over? It is never over. That's what a cycle does. It repeats.

In response to the 2008 credit collapse, Congress passed the *Dodd-Frank Wall Street Reform and Consumer Protection Act.* This 2010 legislation was quite a dance for the politicians and bankers, with music provided by the banking lobby band. In fairness, Dodd-Frank appears to provide for an orderly liquidation in the event a mega bank blows up its portfolio and becomes insolvent. This mountain of busy-work regulations is Congress's answer to the bailout syndrome and an attempt to end the moral hazard of investing other people's money, while expecting government help after a major failure. We will see what changes are ahead and if such worthy ends survive the next financial crisis and future administrations.

It's no wonder the banking system seems unstable. Just look at the way laws have changed at the ideological whim of the politicians in power, regardless of party affiliation. Maybe it's just consistently bad advice from an economics profession that is trying to be something it's not. Constructing abstract mathematical models and ignoring the history of the economy and the evidence before your eyes gives a modern meaning to counting angels on the head of a pin. Our high priests of the economy seem to need a wake up call. Maybe that's what's coming next.

Now the tide is trying to turn from deregulation to reregulation and the process may start again. Regulation neither creates stability nor properly allocates capital for economic growth. A more effective solution is proper incentives that allow the market to operate within the rule of law without legalized corruption and predictable fraud.

What do we know and what surprises can we expect? Banks and their lobbyists are firmly in control of Congress. Over-the-counter derivatives are not traded on open exchanges, which would promote transparency and free market price discovery. Given this, you might say nothing of significance has changed and we are in for more of the same financial turmoil. It is a bit of irony that those yelling the loudest for deregulation and free markets are the first to run to government for help when they get in trouble. That shouldn't be a surprise next time. Now let's look at the timing schedule for the next crisis.

How to Apply Cycles to Real Estate

The defining factor in real estate cycles is activity. During the expansion phase, there is more buying and selling activity. During the contraction phase, activity seems to drop off a cliff. At their core, cycles are timing guidelines for changes in real estate market activity and in the general economy as well. An increase in demand for goods and services is an expansion in gross domestic product (GDP). A decrease in demand is a contraction in GDP, which is one factor in the definition of a recession.

Cycles peak as activity reaches a high point. Cycles bottom as activity reaches a low point. Timing is not always exact, but sometimes a peak will hit the mark and reignite expectations for regular accuracy. Furthermore, it's difficult to remember change is coming when the boom is on and everyone is rolling in cash and confidence. You know it's too good to last, but it just keeps on going. Then little warning signs pop up. You notice people pulling back and activity slowing.

Cycles are tendencies, not absolutes. They provide a time frame for dealing with the consequences of the fundamental changes buffeting the market. We know there will be consequences. We can't know exactly what they will be or exactly when they will occur. But we can learn from history. We can learn the timing of events that have happened in the past and to some degree why they happened. Here is where cycles help. They provide a possible time context for the unknown that is coming. They are red flags on our calendar.

The housing cycle is generally regular. It tends to peak approximately every five to seven years, reaching crests in 1972, 1979, 1986, 1993, 2000, and 2007, with some a little early and some coming later. If this relatively even time spacing recurs, the next peak will be about 2014. This is likely to be nothing more than a little bump on the way down or across the bottom, as was the case on the parabolic way up in 2000. In that year, the normal correction was muted by low interest rates and lax loan underwriting standards. This seven-year cycle includes housing starts, housing completions, new home sales, existing home sales, all of which cluster in peaks every five to seven years. Sometimes the peaks are obvious, as in 2007. Sometimes they are barely visible, as in 2000. Charts of housing related activity show these cyclical tendencies.

Of equal importance is the 18-year cycle in general real estate activity. This 18-year rhythm had projected peaks in 1980 and 1999, with troughs projected in 1990 and 2008. The uncanny thing about this cycle is the troughs in 1990 and 2008 hit the bull's eye on the real estate-related savings and loan and banking crises. If we continue the projection, 2026 is the next trough. However, 2017 might be the next high point for general real estate activity. Note that the projected peaks have not been as useful as the projected troughs. The 18-year projections are based on the work of Edward R. Dewey, "The 18-Year Rhythm" in *Cycles: Selected Writings* (Foundation for the Study of Cycles, 1970, p. 343).

One other cyclical tendency coincides with the projected 18-year peak in 2017. There was a 10-year timing pattern of crises in the early 1800s that has resurfaced. In 1987, the stock market crashed. In 1998, Russia defaulted, and Long Term Capital Management failed and almost halted the banking system. In 2008, Lehman and Bear Sterns failed, the commercial loan market froze, and the housing market collapsed, coinciding with the 18-year trough in the real estate cycle. This timing indicates another financial panic in about 2018, if not earlier. It could be the collapse of the secretive over-the-counter derivatives market, failure of a large multinational bank, or a spike in interest rates due to inflation fears. Who knows what will trigger the panic, given all the opportunity and areas for crises these days. However, the consequences are likely to be more severe than 2008, given that not much has changed and debt and contingent liabilities continue to grow throughout the financial system. This 10-year pattern in the first half of the 1800s is noted by Kindleberger: 1816, 1826, 1837, 1847, and 1857. (For more on cycles, see the excellent classic *Manias, Panics and Crashes, A History of Financial Crises*, sixth edition, 2011 by Kindleberger and Aliber.)

The best you can do is to arrange your life so that no matter what happens, your chosen lifestyle will continue. This means avoid debt or at least excessive leverage during this deflationary period. Emphasize cash flow in your acquisitions and don't rely on appreciation alone. Crises are opportunities if you act with awareness and adapt with flexibility. Awareness of cycles can help take the surprise out of major change so you can more easily keep your balance. Therein is the meaning of having a balanced portfolio.

These periodic panics come as no surprise when you know the history of our cyclical investment market and the causes that contribute to normal fluctuations. Remember that extreme speculation is a rush to debt and illiquid assets as prices rise with no end in sight. Extreme panic is when that end is in sight and everyone rushes to sell and get out of debt. Panic is mainly an attempt to regain liquidity by converting to cash and holding on to it. Real estate liquidity is a function of price. So, in extreme circumstances, prices must drop to attract cash. Usually, the lower the price is the more liquid the property is.

Generally, the cyclical process typical of real estate follows the supply-demand dynamics of an industry segment, such as offices, retail and industrial space, apartments, and housing. There are also regional supply-demand forces: a technological boom may be underway in the northeast at the same time an oil-induced depression is going on in the southwest. Real estate is a core component of the expansion and contraction of the general economy which, during the past 150 years, has moved through somewhat regular business cycles that average 51 months from trough to trough. These are basic inventory adjustments and are distinct from the newer financial crises.

Two factors interact to influence the general level of activity in real estate: jobs and credit. Expanding employment opportunity is the primary force behind demand for real estate. More jobs attract more people and new families form. When the job market is contracting, houses go on the market, and retail and office space empties. During a contraction, demand for real estate shrinks as supply grows—not new supply—but offices, stores, and sometimes apartments that were once occupied become vacant, adding to a growing inventory.

Interest rates and the availability of credit are of equal importance to the health of the real estate market. If there are no jobs and few loans available, low interest rates are of little help in stimulating real estate activity. Low interest rates do not mean that credit is available. This is apparent when bankers suddenly discover the importance of maintaining capital requirements and strict underwriting standards and hoard cash to improve their balance sheets.

Worse still is the damage done to commercial property when lenders refuse to roll over loans as fear grips where routine used to rule. A five- or seven-year loan on a commercial building is typical, and rolling the loan over is expected. But, when the bank that owns the loan fails and is acquired by an out-of-town bank that has cash on the mind, refusal to renew becomes a real estate risk.

The Great Continuing Contraction of 2008 may ultimately result in more psychological damage than anyone anticipated. Obviously, it was preceded by speculation in housing and related debt, created in part by government deregulation, with support from a bubble-creating Federal Reserve. This type of policy-based instability wasn't dreamed up over night and won't be corrected without pain. The process of debt liquidation can take a very long time and is likely to damage public acceptance of real estate as a sure-thing investment. An eventual change in attitude will lay the foundation for a new cycle and a new opportunity to acquire real estate for the next long-term cycle of price inflation and the subsequent debt liquidation.

Cycles are just market tendencies that reappear from time to time. Their general regularity is a gift for the alert. Be alert.

1. Maintain a certain portion of investment funds in real estate for long-term appreciation.

2. Avoid highly leveraged acquisitions, and therefore large debt obligations, at the peak of the business cycle.

3. Make long-term real estate investments, which you plan to hold during severe contractions, as nearly free of debt as possible.

4. Use cyclical peaks in the economy as opportunities to sell short-term investments when demand and prices appear to have increased excessively and when public optimism and interest in real estate is high.

5. Pay off debt when cash is easy to get and endeavor to make any loans you sign nonrecourse to avoid personal liability.

How to Recognize and Profit from Speculative Patterns

The speculative increase in prices is a curious process with a long history involving many types of assets. It is curious because the same psychological factors play a major role, regardless of the assets involved or the level of expertise or wealth of the participants. The process is reenacted time and again in different financial arenas without the majority of the participants realizing that they are part of a scenario with a recognizable pattern.

For example, toward the end of the acquisition phase, it is almost as if a buying frenzy takes precedence over reason as buyers acquire more at ever increasing prices in the hope of getting, and the fear of missing, the "sure" profits made by those who bought earlier. Toward the end of the boom, fear of loss crowds out fear of missing a profit and hope of riches, as the specter of repaying the debt used to buy the asset becomes psychologically dominant. Characteristics of the boom-bust process are:

1. Excessive credit expansion. Loans are easy to get when secured by an asset that is rising in price. Funds from the new loans are used to buy more of the speculative asset.

2. Visions of wealth dominate consciousness. Pursuit of "more" takes hold as the participants attempt to expand their holdings and increase their standard of living in line with new-found self-importance and impressions of financial genius.

3. The participants believe they have it made. Confidence takes over. Owners refuse to sell except at very high prices because of the obvious permanent value. At this stage, the press and how-to-get-rich books spread the word of past successes, drawing in the late-comers who buy at high prices with new debt commitments in a topping market.

4. A trigger event stops the market rise, and prices fall of their own weight. The failure of a major bank that has extended credit to buy land to build more housing is one example.

5. Debt pressures mount as participants attempt to sell into a weak market. Fear takes over at this stage as participants worry more about lack of cash to pay loans than missing out on future price increases. Lenders realize their loans are in trouble and try to salvage what they can by working with borrowers, even if it means extending more credit.

6. Debt liquidation begins as foreclosures mount. Assets are taken by the lenders as values drop below the amount of the loans. Loans are written down as no buyers are found. An increasing number of lenders get in trouble, and the government is forced to step in with taxpayers' money. In extreme cases, the process can take years.

7. *Loss of investor confidence eventually follows.* This is the opposite extreme of the blind speculation found at market tops. It is a time to wait and watch for opportunity and the beginning of the recovery when the cycle starts up again. Patience is the key at this stage. Things will get better. They always have. Cycles will continue, bringing both the good and the bad. And after this stage is over, it will be time for the good again.

Extreme speculation tends to involve government intervention to prevent damage to the banking system, which ironically is endangered by prior government action that changed laws, regulations, or interest rates that had held lenders and speculators in check.

Furthermore, the timing of cycles tends to fit with the events that occurred during the previous cycle point, containing many similar if not identical events. The normal flow of economic activity through cycles is the basis for growth and the natural corrections needed by the system. It is also the basis of opportunity for those who are willing to adapt and take advantage of the ebb and flow within the real estate market.

How to Time Acquisitions to Take Advantage of Real Estate Cycles

The natural tendency we all have is to focus attention on isolated events, which form only part of the ongoing real estate cycle. It's very difficult to define and isolate a process until a major terminal event defines it as completed. The beginning of a process is easy to overlook until the process itself ends, often with some dramatic occurrence. For example, the speculative excesses of the housing market in 2004 and 2005 were easy to overlook until prices fell. The process was then framed and obvious. Few people saw it coming and virtually no one initially realized the extent of the fall in prices. Even less obvious was the endemic fraud and lending malfeasance.

Prices boom, then bust, and few see the boom in perspective until the bust is in place. As all can now admit, real estate is not exempt from this process. It just moves more slowly as a market and lacks rapid price quotes. But real estate prices do rise and fall. And that cyclical activity is the basis of opportunity.

One way to frame the events that constitute a real estate cycle is to look for general activity while it is underway, realizing that it is part of a larger cycle.

There are four activity stages that define the real estate cycle:

1. Activity basing. Real estate activity is low as excess supply is very gradually absorbed. Sellers give concessions, which amount to lower prices. Public expectations reach a low point. Liquidity is the prime concern, cash is in demand, and risk avoidance dominates investor psychology.

2. Activity rising. Interest in real estate picks up as demand begins to absorb the existing supply. Prices rise, terms tighten, and construction activity starts up in an attempt to take advantage of growing demand.

3. Activity topping. Supply begins to catch up with demand. Construction activity tapers off, but public awareness of the profit made by others is at a high point. The outlook is generally optimistic, and the greatest fear is missing a profit. New construction hangs on as long as lenders are willing to lend.

4. Activity falling. Too much supply is available for demand. Rents and prices stop rising and sellers are forced to give concessions on terms. Public expectation of profit diminishes as market activity decreases and credit becomes increasingly restrictive. Pessimism increases to balance the previous optimism as investors pull back to avoid risk and reduce debt exposure. After activity falls, the basing stage starts again. Normally, the complete cycle takes years to complete in the slow-moving real estate market. Activity in different segments of the real estate market is a reflection of the combined interaction of supply and demand for a particular type of real estate, whether apartments, offices, retail, or single family housing.

Summary of Cycles

The Business Cycle

This is a measure of the contraction and expansion of gross domestic product (GDP) and more, as determined by a timing committee of economists. It is a ragged cycle, but there is a 150-year history of recessions said to average about 51 months apart.

Recessions: 1970, 1974-75, 1980, 1982, 1991, 2001, 2008-09

The Housing Cycle
Timing is about 5 to 7 years.

Peaks: 1972, 1979, 1986, 1993, 2000, 2007, 2014, 2021, 2028, 2035

The 18.33-Year Real Estate Cycle
Timing seems to hold up so far, with troughs more visible than peaks.

Peaks: 1926.0, 1944.5, 1962.6, 1980.9, 1999.2, 2017.6, 2035.9
Troughs: 1935.2, 1955.5 1971.8, 1990.1, 2008.4, 2026.7, 2045.0

The 10-Year Financial Crisis Cycle
This resurfaced from the early 1800s.

1987, 1998, 2008, 2018, 2028, 2038

Keep in mind that cycles are the result of human behavior and therefore, inexact.

Introduction to 150 Techniques

There are three personality traits that can help you and are worth developing: be flexible, adapt to change, and avoid rigidity. So far, I have recounted many stories about people who have found approaches to real estate acquisition that worked for them. My purpose was to show what is possible. In most cases, I have used the real first names of the people involved because I admired their insights and actions. There is a follow-up to one of the stories that is not so positive but is instructive.

You may remember the story of Paul (not his real name) who acquired over $10 million in apartments by putting on new first mortgages, giving the owner the down payment from the proceeds, and asking the owner to carry a second. This is a very effective technique. But the debt must be managed. To manage it requires balance and awareness of the big picture. These are personal qualities; not mathematical calculations. Paul was a mathematician.

Several years into his apartment acquisition activity, a recession hit the economy and vacancies increased in one of Paul's larger complexes. Paul had rules. One of them was that each complex must stand on its own and pay its own debt. As the vacancy in this larger complex grew, it became impossible to pay the second lien with the rent generated by that particular complex. As the payments on the second fell behind, Paul's staff pleaded with him to pay it from other income, which he had. Stubborn investor that he was, he refused. This is a quality that may have helped him in negotiations. But now it was time for him to look inside and find other qualities to deal with the new reality he faced. He couldn't. Rules are rules. Math has rules.

I have a vision of him sitting alone in court listening to the judge rule against him. One deficiency judgment and liens on his other property was all it took to destroy the good planning and business he had built in a few short years. His loss was the outcome of personal rigidity.

This follow-up story to initial success is instructive because it tells us all to be aware of our own traits and to be watchful for ways they may hold us back or get us in trouble. Personal rigidity has hurt many. But there is a way around it.

I remember reading years ago about the first westerner to win the full contact martial arts world championship held in Thailand. He struggled for years to find the skill to accomplish this significant goal. In an interview after the fight quoted in a small news item, he said he finally learned to get out of his own way.

Real estate simply exists. The opportunity presented by real estate is what we do with it. The techniques are ways we can do things with real estate to increase our financial security when we learn to get out of our own way.

Chapter Six

Techniques for Acquiring Real Estate without Cash

Knowing what is possible gives you the opportunity to accelerate real estate acquisition. If you learn what others have done, you simply increase your chances by drawing on their knowledge. The purpose behind the following techniques is to give you the advantage that comes from knowing specific ways to overcome barriers.

Some of the techniques may solve an immediate problem and pave the way for closing an acquisition that you've had your eye on for some time. Others will not fit your needs today, but someday they may. The objective is to give you the widest possible range of alternatives to choose from. Look at these techniques as the starting point. They are meant to be modified. Try to combine and customize them to fit your specific needs.

It's what you do with a technique that counts. Some have applications to several different situations. The application is more important than the structure of the technique. For that reason, I have included applications for the same technique in more than one situation. Look at each application as a variation of one or more technique. The purpose is to provoke thought that will help you find a way to acquire property. These techniques are ideas that have been put to use. And as Melinda always says, "The cool thing about ideas is they lead to new ideas."

Always consult a lawyer for legal guidance because laws change and correctly completed documentation is a requirement. Because tax laws change, always use an accountant to avoid tax liability surprises.

1. Mortgage Out. By definition, you mortgage out when the permanent loan is equal to or larger than total acquisition costs.

The mathematical key is to keep land and construction costs at the same percentage of appraised value as the financing. With existing projects, the sales price must equal the loan value of the property, which means the sales price is lower than the appraisal.

Mortgaging out is probably the most valued objective of builders and developers. Meeting this elusive objective requires a combination of cost control and solid tenants. Developers have found mortgaging out difficult as land and construction costs have climbed. Nevertheless, rents have also moved up, and with a shrewd approach, you can still build value into certain projects that will make it work. Development is defined as creating value beyond the cost of development. Mortgaging out is a realization of created value. The ease of this technique is to a large degree dependent on the credit cycle. Easy credit means ease of implementation.

Rents need to be high enough to generate an income approach appraisal that is comfortably above costs. Since lenders primarily base their estimate of value on the income-producing ability of the property, you have an inherent chance for success. Everything from ranches to shopping centers has been acquired using this technique. The objective is to keep costs of land and construction to about 70 or 80 percent of appraisal, depending on the percentage of value you will receive from the loan.

Investors who have an inventory of commercial land acquired years ago have a definite advantage. Land that was acquired just a few years ago is more likely to contribute to appraised value in excess of the original cost. But there are a couple of alternatives if land costs are high. Negotiate a long-term land lease with low payments at the outset to give you the margin for borrowing the initial development money. Include an option to buy the land. Another possibility is to start in small towns where land values are lower.

Big name, rated tenants and a shopping center developer and builder who can leave profit in the project add to the ease of mortgaging out. Holding construction costs down is essential in any case.

2. Refinance with the Seller Carrying Back a Second. This technique is a natural for acquiring older property (especially apartments) that can be refinanced. Here, the primary objective is to obtain a new first mortgage large enough to pay both the existing loans and the down payment required by the seller. The down payment actually comes from the proceeds of the new first mortgage.

The balance of the sales price is then carried by the seller on a second mortgage. It may also be possible to structure the terms of the transaction so that a portion of the loan proceeds can be used for renovation of the property. The proceeds of the new loan meet three objectives:

1. To pay the existing loans
2. To make the down payment
3. To upgrade the property

As with most acquisition techniques, this one works smoothly when the seller wants out and trusts your management ability. The challenge here is to convince the seller to accept a totally financed acquisition. It is equally important to build enough value into the loan presentation to get the largest possible first mortgage. This requires a very complete presentation of the improvements planned for the property, the benefits of the management system that will be implemented, and the steps that will be taken to increase the rental income. The objective is to convince the seller and lender that you are the best possible buyer and their interests will be better cared for when you own the property.

There are a couple of direct benefits to the seller: and

1. He steps out of the liability of the existing loans;
2. He gets the down payment he wants from the proceeds of the new loan.

Since he was probably prepared to carry back a second position anyway, nothing fundamental has changed. The main negotiating block may concern the amount of the second mortgage. But this need not be a problem if the seller has confidence in the income-producing potential of the property and your ability to manage it professionally.

3. Create Paper. Real estate equity is buying power. And in times of high inflation, it is a source of capital appreciation, which is the best chance for keeping your estate even with or ahead of inflation. Creating paper is a method of using the purchasing power of your home or other real estate equity without refinancing or selling.

The mechanics of this approach are simple. You sign a note, usually payable in monthly installments, which is secured by a second mortgage on real estate you own. You give the new note to the seller. The note buys out the seller's equity in the property you are acquiring. It is the down payment. If you default on the note, the seller gets your other property. As added security, the terms could be written so that in the event of default, the seller would get the property he sold as well.

Of course, you would not want to use this technique if there were the least possibility of default. The income must be there to support the payments. Using your residence as security can be a means of ensuring the seller that the note for the down payment will be paid. A personal note backed with solid collateral that meets the income needs of the seller can make more sense than cash, especially if interest rates are low and you are willing to offer a relatively high rate. The challenge is to meet the seller's desire for security. Using a residence as security for the note is designed to meet this need.

4. Refinance Your Home. The steady, unrelenting increase in single family home values from 1980 to 2000 was probably a major factor contributing to the easy credit and over speculation ending in the mid 2000s and the financial panic of 2008. That doesn't mean the market for home investment is over. It takes more than a few misguided politicians, wild-eyed bankers, and overly optimistic house buyers to end the American dream. The equity in a home that grows each month as a result of paying the loan and from natural demand is still recognized as money in the bank. Home ownership has replaced savings, often by necessity rather than by choice. It's difficult to save money unless you make a lot of it. In our "inflation in what you need and deflation in what you don't need," cash flow extraction society, an extra dollar to save is hard to find. Savings accounts pay little, so it's easy to understand why paying cash into home equity provides greater benefit. However, cash reserves are always important and worth sacrificing for.

Recognition of home equity as savings security moved

housing that used to be viewed as a consumer item into the area of acceptable low-risk investment and necessary inflation hedge. You can turn home equity into cash by refinancing, adding a second mortgage or a home equity loan and use it to acquire additional investment real estate. It is also a chance to become overextended. But with prudent planning and financial analysis, home equity can be a safe source of investment capital.

The challenge here is to put the tax-free cash to work earning investment dollars. Using the refinance proceeds for consumer goods doesn't make sense, since no income or capital gains are produced to repay the debt. The obvious requirement is that the benefits of the real estate acquired with the refinance proceeds be sufficient to offset the risk of additional debt on such an important personal asset. Carefully weigh the balance between risk and reward before using this approach.

5. Professional Services as Down Payment. If you don't have cash, what do you have? That is the basic question to thoroughly explore as you negotiate any acquisition. Often the answer falls back on what you can do that is of benefit to the seller.

Sellers who really want to get out and avoid getting back in will often look to your management ability. Just knowing that their equity will be protected by good management and that they will eventually be paid from the improved operating efficiency of the property can be enough to swing the deal. If you can provide this kind of assurance and add another benefit, you may be in good shape.

Do you have a professional skill the seller might need that would meet part of or the entire down payment requirement? For example, if the seller is interested in the stock market and you are a computer programmer, how about creating a program to trade stocks or test his system and monitor the transactions?

Lawyers and doctors have an advantage with this technique because of the high costs of these professions. Furthermore, eventually almost everyone seems to need their services. Contractors and related building trades also have an edge because real estate sellers often have other property that may need work. This is a natural opportunity to trade for the down payment.

Knowing the seller is often half the battle. If you have an idea of what he wants out of life, you may be able to jump the cash gap and go directly to the objective. There are probably several things any seller will do with the cash he has, whether it comes from a down payment or his job. What can you provide without the intermediate step of cash?

6. Effort Equity. If you are putting a partnership together for real estate acquisition, a percentage of the ownership may be appropriate compensation. It is often an expected incentive that is built into the project from the beginning.

The purpose of this technique is for you to receive credit toward the down payment for the value of the effort you contribute to the property or project. In complex investment transactions, it is usually one person who creates the idea for a real estate transaction and puts the pieces together that result in a closed transaction. Without this type of effort, few deals would close. More often than not, the value of the property is enhanced as a result. When this is done for the benefit of a partnership, it is only appropriate that the creating member be compensated for the extra effort. Equity in the property is one solid form of compensation. It is also a method of increasing the likelihood of a profitable outcome when the partners look to the same person for management and ultimate sale of the property.

Real estate brokers who work with out-of-town investors have an advantage. There is a degree of added comfort when you know someone is on site who will stand behind the property and work out the problems. A right to participate in ownership makes good business sense when the primary owner depends on your effort for his profit.

7. Borrow Against Paper. If you own second mortgages, trust deeds, or real estate contracts secured by property you have previously sold, consider using this paper as collateral for acquisition funds. A second mortgage is a decaying *debt* investment. Real property is normally considered an appreciating *equity* investment. Borrowing against decaying paper to buy appreciating income property is a method of converting the asset to cash without disposing of it.

As payments are received on your paper-collateral, they are

applied directly to repayment of the acquisition loan. The value stored in the paper which was formerly diminishing with each principal payment and each jump in inflation is now stored in an appreciating investment. The transition step is to borrow against the paper to generate the cash necessary to meet the down payment requirements of the seller. The net effect of the procedure is reinvestment of a portion of your capital gain while deferring the tax on the balance that would be due if you sold the paper.

The amount you can borrow against secured paper will depend somewhat on your relationship with the lender. Standard practice uses about 50 percent of the face value of the paper as a rule-of-thumb. The amount may vary up or down based on your equity and lien position. The condition and value of the property securing the paper will also be a factor. You may be able to borrow more if the property securing the paper is an attractive investment and if you have a position that will allow a quick discount sale in the event of default.

This technique is based on the principle of moving the value you have to the property you want. You just hitch a ride on borrowed cash to make the move.

8. Seller Pays Buyer. It may be a surprise that a seller of real estate would actually pay someone to buy property. But when you consider the spectrum of human behavior, the scenario leading to this technique is not difficult to understand. The instances in which I have seen this happen were both large properties with correspondingly large debt. Sellers were anxious to get out from under the obligations and use their energies in more productive pursuits. Furthermore, it was going to take some cash to turn the performance of the properties around.

In some cases, your most cooperative negotiator is an overextended property owner who doesn't have the expertise or inclination to deal with real estate that is losing money, becoming a drain on other income and threatening other healthy assets. Cooperation can even extend to providing the cash necessary to offset the risk he is transferring to the buyer. Cases like this illustrate that all real estate is not necessarily appropriate for all investors. In any event, this technique allows an owner to get out of a bad situation that could be damaging his health.

The cash advanced by the seller may, by necessity, be put back into the property to finance the changes needed to make it productive. This cash outlay by the seller is not necessarily a negotiated gift. It can also be structured as a loan secured by the acquired property. Consequently, the seller can act as lender, selling to someone who can do the job and financing the effort to do it. There are situations in real estate as in general business, which require an infusion of cash to operate productively. A seller who puts up money to protect his equity and other assets may be making a good business move.

9. Acquire with Future Profits. If you are going into a project that has doubtful cash flow, this technique can balance part of the risk. It is a deferred down payment method tied to the profitability of the acquired property.

The value of the target property may be there based on comparable sales and replacement cost analysis, but it may lack the income to justify the owner's equity requirement. The source of the income problem may be poor management, a lack of demand, or a mistake in the design of the property, such as inadequate parking. Regardless of the cause, you should see a ready solution before taking on the problem.

This is the type of opportunity that will allow you to negotiate your way into ownership and pay for it by virtue of your entrepreneurial and management skills. As the property begins to show a net profit above a predetermined monthly amount, the seller receives a payment toward his equity. Every dollar above the agreed-upon monthly minimum goes to the seller. The faster you turn the property around, the faster the seller is paid. He shares the risk by waiting for payment until the property produces.

The objective is to give you enough margin to make a losing investment a producer without the pressure and risk of laying out a cash down payment. It is a method of making a property pay its own way while giving the right buyer an incentive to make sure the job gets done.

10. Acquire with Closing Credits. This is an approach that uses time to your direct advantage.

When you buy toward the end of the tax year but before

property taxes are due, and a few days after the rent on the property is due, you are in line for certain cash benefits. Although the net effect may depend on the type of loan you're assuming, the proration of taxes and rents will usually reduce the amount of cash needed to close.

When you close after a significant portion of the year has passed during which the seller was liable for property taxes, you will be credited with the amount of the seller's tax liability. Then when the property tax bills come due, you will pay them directly for the entire year. Until the tax bills are due, you have use of that money. The routine at closing is to credit the tax liability against the cash required for the down payment.

Of equal importance is the proration of rents. When you close a few days after the rent is due, you will usually receive credit for the balance of the rent representing the remaining days in the month. You own the property as of the day of closing, so you get the rent for the rest of the month. Timing your purchase and planning the routine math in your favor can significantly reduce the cash due at closing and often entirely eliminate it when combined with other techniques. Always figure out your net cash due at closing *after proration* before deciding you don't have enough money for a down payment.

11. Assign the Rents. When you are borrowing the down payment from a bank and need additional security, this approach may help. The income stream from property is itself a source of security. It has value and can be used as loan collateral.

If the terms of the existing loans do not indicate that the rents have previously been assigned, you are past the first barrier. All you need is an "assignment of rents" agreement drawn by a knowledgeable real estate lawyer and a loan officer willing to accept it as backup for a signature loan. A properly written assignment gives the lender the right to impound the rents to pay the loan in the event of default. This added security for the down payment loan may just be the edge required to satisfy the banker.

Of course, you are negotiating what is essentially a commercial signature loan, and the bank will normally look at your total financial statement and credit history in making the decision. Any form of security will simply make the chances of success that much better. By assigning the rents, the bank has additional collateral to meet the ever-present need of satisfying bank examiners. This is a requirement every loan officer must keep in mind. When you know ways to beef up the security for a loan, it is that much easier for a loan officer to help you. Keep in mind that a cash-flow history and projections on the property are required backup material when you are applying for any loan, regardless of the security you offer.

I remember talking with a banker who told me how much he enjoyed working with the buyers in our transaction because they made his job so much easier. Bob had graduated from a respected university with a major in real estate and always made a complete spreadsheet that projected the performance he anticipated from the acquisition property. This meant that the banker had to do less work to get the loan through the various bank committees.

12. Acquire with a Repair Partnership. Property that needs rehabilitation may be a headache for the owner but it is an opportunity for you to put together a repair partnership. Start by determining potential partners who have skills that will upgrade the property. A plumber, an electrician, a carpenter, and other needed tradesmen contribute their work toward the down payment. Each receives a percentage of ownership equal to the value of the work contributed. The improvements increase the property's value, thereby replacing the seller's need for evidence that the buyers won't default.

The seller takes his equity on a purchase money mortgage and in effect has greater security by virtue of the property improvements than he would have with a cash down payment. The work done by the partners serves as security to the seller. It demonstrates that the buyers have put value into the property. The sales price can even be negotiated upward to reflect the added value as a result of the renovation contributions if necessary. This would increase the face amount of the purchase money mortgage.

There is also a way of determining the sales price based on the rehabilitation costs. If the work contributed by the partners represents 20 percent of the ultimate market value of the property after repairs, the sales price would then be 80 percent of that figure. Consequently, the note and mortgage to the seller is 80 percent of the eventual value, which may be more or less than the original asking price.

Sometimes the only way to save a property from going downhill is to bring it back up with an infusion of long overdue repairs. A seller who realizes this may ultimately come out ahead and avoid the serious loss that could otherwise occur if the deterioration of the property had not been stopped. Deferred maintenance is a common problem with rentals. This is one way to turn the problem into an advantage.

13. The Note Partnership. Several small notes signed by a number of individuals can be better security than one large note signed by one person. Ten $9,000 notes from different people, each having a net worth of $90,000, is sounder security than a note from one person with a net worth equal to the face value of the note. Acquisition partnerships that realize the negotiation advantage of buying as a group can be quite successful.

An additional advantage to this method is the flexibility it provides the seller. If she needs cash from time to time, she can discount and sell one of the notes without stepping into a tax liability for the entire profit because installment reporting might be protected.

Security for the notes can be handled in a couple of ways. A mortgage on the acquired property could serve as security for all the notes. Another approach is to have each of the partners secure his note by a separate mortgage placed on different property owned outside the partnership. For example, individual residences may prove to be better collateral in the eyes of the seller than the property sold.

If the property acquired is used to secure the notes, it is important to word the documents so a default by one partner would trigger default of the entire property. This is to protect the seller. The notes and mortgage should also be written to protect the other partners by giving them the right to step in and cure a default by one of the other members. Negotiating a no-cash acquisition can sometimes be accomplished more easily by spreading the liability (and security) among several people.

14. Advertise for a Private Loan. This method of raising

acquisition capital proves that you never really know what is possible until you try. Venture capital provided by individuals and privately owned companies has historically been the foundation of new business. It is no different in real estate. One young real estate entrepreneur turned a steady credit line provided by a wise and trusting widow into a multimillion dollar company. The right kind of financial backing has helped more than one hard-working person to the top, and it can happen to you.

If you have found what seems to be one of those rare opportunities that comes along when you are least prepared financially, consider advertising for a private loan. With a project that has potential, you can offer higher-than-usual interest and a percentage of the profits if necessary. You may be surprised at the response if your ad request clearly reflects the unique opportunity you perceive in the property.

There are people with money who know a good opportunity when they see one. It is understandable that they would want more than an average return for their willingness to accept the risks. You may already know someone or a company that specializes in what is traditionally considered high-risk venture capital lending. If you do, it may not be necessary to advertise. But if you don't, why not try an ad? Many cities have a small group of business people who regularly meet to hear presentations for new ventures. Your presentation could be worth their time. In any event, only deal with people who are established in your community and are known for honesty.

15. Commission as Down Payment. This acquisition technique illustrates one of the real benefits of being a licensed real estate agent. I have met people who have entered the real estate brokerage business mainly because of the commission benefit when they acquire property for their own account.

Being active in the real estate brokerage business puts you in the middle of the action where you can see opportunities while they are still forming. And you can cut the cost of entry by the amount of your own fee when you buy for your own account.

Real estate commissions are generally paid in cash at closing of the transaction. The net effect of paying a commission is to reduce both the sales price and the cash received by the seller.

Conversely, when a broker invests for his own account, the net effect of receiving a commission is reduction of both the price and cash required for down payment.

From a practical standpoint, this technique is applied during negotiation to eliminate the unnecessary payment and repayment of cash between buyer and seller. There is really no need to run the commission through the hands of the escrow agent from the buyer to the seller as down payment and back to the buyer in the form of commission. The obvious alternative is to agree during negotiation to reduce the sales price by the amount of the commission and deduct it from the cash down payment.

16. Credit Union Loan. Members of credit unions have an inside track for getting an acquisition loan. Furthermore, the interest rate and terms are often easier to digest than those of the neighborhood bank.

Credit unions exist for the benefit of the members. It is really a different relationship than is possible with a bank, especially a big bank. The ownership structure of a bank is less personal, and the objectives of profit and growth are different. Credit union membership requirements have become increasingly relaxed over the years. It should be considered among your first sources for an acquisition loan.

The process is similar to that of a bank. It is easier sometimes because of the relationships among the credit union, your job, and your employer. There is less risk from the credit union's point of view because they know you have a job and the degree of your security in that job.

The amount of the loan and the type of collateral, if any, will vary based on your income and the money you have on deposit with the credit union. But the point is that the credit union is there for your benefit, and using it for real estate acquisition capital is one of the best ways to get the benefit.

17. Real Estate Equity as Down Payment. This technique is a form of real estate exchange with an amazing number of applications. For our purposes, though, it is useful in developing a somewhat different view of the ways you can use the real estate you currently own. Equity in real estate is one of the most effective forms of purchasing power available to investors today. It can be a tax-free, inflation-resistant, and relatively liquid asset when you know the variety of exchange techniques available.

When certain legal requirements are met, you can exchange investment real estate for different investment real estate without paying tax on the gain. This special real estate opportunity is provided by Section 1031 of the Internal Revenue Code and has a number of variations.

For example, a larger investment property may suit your growth and appreciation objectives better than the property you now own. This is the simple basis for an exchange. In an exchange, the equity of the current property serves as the down payment for the acquired property. If you receive no cash or other consideration and assume larger loans, there is no tax on the disposition of the original property. This tax advantage alone makes exchanging mandatory in many cases. Why sell and pay tax then reinvest when you can exchange tax free?

In addition, using the exchange process to build an estate eliminates the need to raise cash. The erroneous objection that has stopped some exchanges is the assumption that the owner of the property you want doesn't want your property. You never know until you try. And even if the seller won't accept your property, there is an easy and routine method of structuring an exchange for you and a sale for the other owner. One approach is to sign an agreement to exchange, contingent on the sale of your property out of escrow. There are strict guidelines that must be followed (see IRS Publication 544 for details).

Using the real estate you have to acquire the real estate you want makes good sense when the alternative is selling, paying tax, and buying with the money you have left over.

18. Family Loan. Don't overlook the possibility of borrowing from family members to raise the cash you need for a worthwhile investment. How many people have been forced to borrow occasionally from close family to get through difficult times? Borrowing to acquire investment real estate makes a lot more sense in many ways.

When the investment opportunity is unique and liable to slip through your fingers if you don't act fast, consider talking it over with the people who care about you the most. There are a lot of benefits here: no credit check, probably a fast OK, and the loan application can probably be made over the dinner table. You may actually be doing a family friend a favor by providing good security and higher interest than a savings account. Furthermore, giving someone a chance to help you is often more rewarding for them personally than leaving unneeded money in the bank to be chewed away by inflation.

The point here, as with all acquisition techniques, is that you must consider all funding alternatives and combinations of alternatives, and borrowing among family is one of the most often-used and successful.

19. Acquisition with Soft Paper. Soft paper refers to loans that have low initial payments. The terms can be structured for interest only at the beginning, with an increased principal reduction later. The term of the loan is also lengthened in certain cases to meet the objective of this technique, which is to "soften" the impact of the payments on the buyer. Therefore, when you acquire real estate with soft paper, the transaction is set up to make the monthly payments easier.

High prices have forced many lenders to accept longer term financing for new car loans and lower initial payments on government-sponsored and conventional home loans. This continuing institutional trend has made soft paper more easily accepted in privately financed real estate negotiations. In the past, soft paper was normally used on purchase money mortgages when prices ran up and credit tightened. Now it is the only way many people can afford a car or home.

Soft paper allows acquisition of property even when the price is higher than the property's income can support under a conventional lending situation. When the seller is adamant about price but not concerned about when he gets it, soft paper can often make the deal workable. If you can pay the asking price, although high, by making the down payment with a soft second mortgage, it is possible to come out ahead in the long run, provided it is done during an inflationary cycle.

Although finding a good real estate deal is the major issue, getting control of it is equally challenging. Property priced at the top price for today's value may be cheap after a few years' appreciation, but it won't do you any good if you cannot gain control today. Try paying the full price with a low-interest, low-payment second mortgage that the income can support. Be sure to cover your risk by avoiding personal liability. In the event of default, limit the seller to repossession of the property. If you think it shows enough promise to warrant paying top dollar and the seller also thinks it is that valuable, there should be little worry about default. And if there is concern about losing it, maybe you should look for another deal.

20. Acquire with a First and Second Then Sell the First for Cash. If you are negotiating the acquisition of free and clear property and the seller wants more cash than you have, this is a good method for supplying it.

First mortgages are more easily sold and are discounted less than second mortgages. In this cashless approach, the seller receives two purchase money mortgages: a first mortgage and a second. The purchaser pays no cash.

The purchase agreement is contingent on locating a buyer for the first mortgage at a price satisfactory to the seller. The sale of the first mortgage can occur concurrently with acquisition of the property, but it doesn't have to. The seller may get a better price for the mortgage by waiting until it is seasoned. The seller receives the net proceeds from the sale of the first mortgage and keeps the second mortgage. The buyer pays no cash, yet the seller gets the cash he wants.

The purpose of splitting the acquisition between a first and second lien position is to establish a relatively large equity and security position for the buyer of the first mortgage. This will usually reduce the discount necessary to sell the paper.

If the seller doesn't like the idea of discounting the sales price by virtue of the first mortgage sale, make up the difference by increasing the amount of the second mortgage. Just increase the face amount of the second by the amount of the discount and work in an equal discount amount for an early pay-off of the second. Another alternative is to compensate the seller for the discount by adding periodic balloon payments in addition to the regular monthly payments on the second. The point is to negotiate whatever is necessary to gain control of the property, provided the eventual profit warrants the risk.

21. Collateral Security Agreement. If an owner will not sell without a down payment because she is worried about "getting the property back," this approach may serve to quiet the concerns. Offer to buy the property with no cash down on a purchase money second. In addition, offer to secure performance on the second by using other property you own as collateral.

The equity value of the collateral property should at least equal the amount of the down payment previously requested. You get in for no cash and the seller gets the security needed to offset fears about getting the property back.

The security agreement should be properly drawn by a lawyer and tied to the payment of the mortgage on the property you are acquiring. It should provide for transfer of the collateral to the seller if you default. It should also provide for release of the additional collateral when the second is paid down to a certain figure. For example, you might include a provision that automatically releases the collateral property when the mortgage is reduced by an amount equal to the down payment the seller had originally requested.

Another alternative is to provide for release of the collateral when the acquired property exceeds a certain value as verified by independent appraisal. Calculation of the release provision under this formula is based on the percentage relationship between the new owner's equity and the balance of the loans. When the balance of the mortgage is 75 percent of the property value, it is in effect the same as making a 25 percent down payment.

22. Borrow Against Your Trust. If you are fortunate to have money that is tied up in a trust, consider the possibility of borrowing against it. You may not be able to bust the trust and you may not want to. But if you have located investment real estate and need to raise acquisition funds, this is one approach.

Bank trust departments often have a difficult time making money on their investments, much less keeping up with inflation or matching the performance of real estate. Taking a hard-nosed business look at what the trust department is doing to your money may be a good idea anyway. You may find that a move to investment real estate is long overdue.

Trusts generally must meet certain liquidity requirements. This makes trust assets excellent collateral. Also there is usually an attempt to balance the portfolio with income-producing assets like blue chip stocks and bonds that have no aura of risk attached to them. Consequently, there are two advantages to borrowing against a trust. You have liquid assets that can usually be converted to cash within a few days and you have income that can be applied toward reducing the money you borrow.

If you can borrow based on your trust income now to acquire income-producing and appreciating real estate, you may improve the effective utility of the trust portfolio and your financial position when you finally do gain full control.

23. Land Sale Lease-Back. Land is the true source of real estate appreciation. Temporarily, improvements may cost more due to inflation, but eventually they will waste away. Insurance companies have recognized this long-term value of land and acquire land under well-located commercial income properties. This growing acceptance of the pivotal role of land values in the economic future is the basis for an effective acquisition technique.

With certain types of property, you can raise down payment funds by setting up a land sale lease-back. The process involves arranging a sale of the land under the improvements you're acquiring and leasing it back. The land sale is made prior to closing, subject to the existing first mortgage. This provides protection for the new landowner by allowing him to step in if there's a default on either the mortgage or the land lease. The proceeds from the land sale go to the seller of the property as down payment to cash out his equity.

Consequently, you in effect acquire a leasehold interest without cash. You receive the direct benefit from rental income and tax shelter for the life of the lease.

Although you are giving up fee ownership with this approach, you may be making a transaction not otherwise possible. There is also the possibility of another benefit. Depending on the mathematics of the transaction, you may be able to sell the land for more than the necessary down payment and pocket the difference.

This technique is generally suitable only for larger transactions that have appeal to real estate investment trusts and other large institutional investors with long-range appreciation in mind.

24. The Lease Down Payment. When you are buying from someone who is both owner and tenant of the property, this technique can help offset the down payment. Consider offering the seller use of the property as down payment. If he plans to keep his business in the same location anyway, you have an opportunity to cover part of the down payment. Essentially, you trade a short-term lease for the down payment.

The seller gets continuing use of his established business location for the term of the lease instead of a cash down payment. You get the property with all its burdens and benefits but without the outlay of cash.

The purpose of this technique is to make a direct move between buyer and seller without the unnecessary step of running cash through the hands of the buyer, then to the seller, and back to the buyer again. Furthermore, if you can negotiate beneficial use of the rent before you receive it, you pick up a time value advantage which makes the rent worth more when applied in a lump sum to the down payment than it was when received monthly.

25. The Installment Down Payment. This technique allows you to acquire property now but pay the seller's equity by making installment payments as you raise the cash. The income from the acquired property offsets the down payment installments, permitting you to avoid a lump sum cash outlay at closing.

For example, if you negotiate quarterly down payment installments of $3,000 and the cash flow is $500 per month, your net out-of-pocket cost will be only $1,500 per quarter. The installment payments are secured by placing a purchase-money second mortgage on the acquisition property. As an alternative, consider negotiating an unsecured personal note payable to the seller.

This method can be helpful when you need time to raise a down payment but have competition for the property from other buyers. A pipeline to commercial loan funds won't do any good if the property is bought out from under you. Tying it down by offering a deferred down payment arrangement is far better than missing a good buy. Lenders and other funding sources often can't move as fast as needed to maintain a competitive stance in moving markets.

26. Assume the Mortgage and the Seller Keeps the Land. This technique permits the seller to retain the long-term benefits of land appreciation while realizing the income benefits of selling the improvements. The seller keeps the land under the improvements instead of receiving a down payment.

There are several ways to structure this acquisition method that allow variation in the negotiations to fit the details of the property. The buyer's primary objective is to acquire the income and tax benefits of ownership by leaving the long-term land benefits to the seller. Retaining land ownership with lease income can be quite an incentive to the seller. Of course, the incentive for you is acquisition of sheltered income without cash.

Although this is technically a leasehold acquisition, you do assume the existing loans and all the burdens and benefits except land ownership. One key to negotiating the offer is to split the asking price between the land and improvement values appropriately. An imbalance between the two is not desirable. Any difference between the land value and the balance of the existing loans would be paid on a purchase-money second mortgage.

It is conceivable that you may end up making three monthly payments: the first mortgage, the purchase-money second, and the land lease. Obviously, it is important to make sure that the income is there to meet the payments. After all, this technique is designed to acquire tax-sheltered cash flow. A real danger in any leased land acquisition is the escalation clause, which is generally negotiated by the seller. It is worth a fight to keep any lease payment increase to a minimum.

27. The Executive Incentive Plan. If you work for a successful privately owned company, the solution to your real estate acquisition program may be at the office. Incentive programs have long been recognized as essential to maximum employee performance. This fact of business life combines with the inflation hedge benefits of real estate to form this technique.

There are several ways to work this cashless acquisition method into a company incentive program. In one case an insurance agency had trouble attracting and keeping good salesmen. In an attempt to provide an incentive, the owner set up an inter-company real estate sharing program. The company acquired a large office building and arranged for sales staff ownership participation, which increased to a certain percentage based on time with the company. If an employee left without working a defined time period, he forfeited ownership in the building. The sales staff grew and made monthly income while building an appreciating net worth because of the foresight of this creative businessman.

Another approach to this acquisition formula is founded on individual employee initiative. If you have a secure relationship with your employer, consider asking to use the company credit line to back up your signature for a down payment loan. Both private and institutional lenders look favorably on loans that are backed by successful corporations. Any loan agreement of this sort should provide for release of the security held against the property when an appropriate principal reduction is made.

28. The 100 Percent Solution. One of the most straightforward ways to acquire real estate without cash is to assume the existing first mortgage and execute a second-position purchase money mortgage for the entire amount of the seller's equity. If the seller does not need cash and is satisfied with your track record, a second mortgage secured by his property may be all that is needed to make the deal. This technique is especially designed for sellers who have faith in their property and its future income potential.

A frequent application of this technique occurs when the seller just wants out and is willing to take what equity he has on paper. In this type of situation, the purchase money mortgage you offer has more value to the seller than his property. There are more benefits in not owning some property for some sellers than owning it, regardless of the potential you may see in it. This opportunity usually follows depressed markets and is a rare find in high growth areas.

It is a fact of real estate that you are better off not making assumptions about what a seller will do. If you want a certain property, you owe it to yourself to offer to buy it any way you can. Anybody with experience in real estate acquisition will tell you that it is filled with more surprises than you could possibly anticipate, and many of them will be in your favor.

29. The Performance Second. The performance second is used in various applications, including acquisitions with and without cash. It is a test of the seller's faith in the value he places on his property.

With this approach, you agree to pay the seller's asking price but make the payments on the second-purchase money mortgage contingent on the income of the property. The selling price is calculated based on the return that the seller represents you will realize from the property. Consequently, you are asking the seller to share your estimate of risk since you are accepting his estimate of value.

If the cash flow is not there, the seller doesn't get paid on the purchase money second mortgage. But if the property performs as the seller represents it will, the payment is made for that month. As an incentive to accept this performance-based payment method, you can negotiate an increase in the payments if the property is more profitable than the seller projected. Setting it up this way allows you and the seller to benefit if he is right. The main purpose is to protect you from overpriced deals by tying the down payment to the property's performance.

Of course, to measure the income fairly, you must separate operating and capital expense items so that one-time replacements are amortized over their useful lives rather than charged in a lump sum against a certain month's cash flow. If the seller refuses to cooperate with this approach, you might question the accuracy of the property's performance projections.

30. Broker as Lender. If you are working with a successful broker, don't overlook the possibility of approaching her as a lending source.

When you consider that the broker will receive a commission from the down payment provided the deal goes through, you can see the stake in the success of the negotiations. Maybe your broker doesn't have an immediate need for the cash from the commission other than finding a high-return investment.

By giving her the opportunity to lend you the cash to make the deal, you both benefit. The broker generates income and places it in a debt investment at the same time. When the alternative is failure because of a cash shortfall, an aggressive broker will usually at least consider lending a helping hand. And for a real estate broker, there's no better payoff than saving a transaction that almost slips away.

31. The Hidden Cosigner. If you have found a good investment property, you have the most difficult job behind you. When you reach this point, don't let not having enough money to close stop the momentum. There is always a method of getting the job done.

One of the most easily overlooked sources of the credit line so essential to real estate acquisition may be closer than you think. If you have located that right deal but the bank won't lend you the money to make the down payment, look for a cosigner. An old friend may be more than interested in helping out. A rich aunt who thinks the world of you may be overjoyed to start you on your way to building an estate. All possibilities must be considered when the alternative is losing a unique real estate buy. It can be a pleasant surprise to find help when you believe in what you are doing.

32. The Insurance Policy Loan. If you have built up cash value in a life insurance policy over the years, consider the direct benefits of borrowing against it to buy real estate. Insurance policy loans are one of the cheapest sources of money around. And borrowing against your cash value is like getting your own money back while using it for loan collateral at the same time.

Furthermore, you provide the best additional collateral possible—your life. And when you think about it, it's hardly a loan. It's really your money which you, in fact, have a right to under the qualifying conditions of the insurance policy. Many young couples have bought their first house when the husband suddenly realized that the insurance policy a friend sold him in college was like money in the bank.

33. Issue Stock. Form a corporation and issue stock to sellers for their equity. It solves the seller's management problems and starts a real estate business for you.

The property owner receives an equity position in the corporation, and the corporation gets an asset. This approach not only reduces the management responsibilities of the owner, but it also provides a degree of diversification.

A real estate corporation with several properties can spread the risks of ownership and increase the possibility that some of the properties will perform profitably.

34. Trade Stock at Purchase Price. Both listed and unlisted stocks and bonds offer a method of acquiring real estate even if the market price of the stock has fallen below the purchase price.

Try trading your stock at the price you paid for it. Who knows, you may find out that the owner has more faith in the stock than in his real estate.

In cases where management requirements are a problem, it is possible that the release from the burdens of ownership would appeal more to the seller than the relative value of the stock.

Furthermore, it is possible that both the property and the stock will increase in value.

35. Signature Loan. One of the most often used methods of acquiring real estate is to borrow the down payment on your signature. The loan is granted based on your ability to repay, given the lender's positive assessment of your employment and overall income.

The objective is to repay a portion of the loan with income from the property and renew it if necessary, eventually repaying it in full with income from the property.

This is essentially a fast method of borrowing money for a good investment opportunity, which uses income from the real estate to repay the loan.

36. Employer Advance. Under the right job conditions, it may prove feasible to borrow or get a salary advance from your employer to use as a down payment. Then use the income from the property and a portion of your salary to pay your employer back.

Of course, this approach requires the right conditions. But an understanding employer may be relieved to lend you money when the alternative is to give you a long overdue salary increase.

Furthermore, your job becomes security for the loan and your loan becomes security for your job. What employer wants to fire an employee and lose the source of repayment for a loan?

37. Credit for Services Certificate. By agreement between buyer and seller, the buyer may reduce the balance of a note held in escrow by sending a credit certificate signed by the seller and buyer, instructing the escrow company to reduce the principal balance by an agreed amount.

For example, a dentist who buys property may make an agreement with the seller to trade dental work for loan reduction payments on owner-carried financing.

This method allows the payment of a note held in escrow with services. It is also a good method of keeping a record of the amount paid by services.

38. Secured Corporate Note. If you are acquiring real estate for your corporation, offer a corporate note secured by specific assets of the corporation, but not secured by the real estate you are acquiring.

Essentially the note becomes the down payment, with additional owner financing secured by the property. In some cases it may be possible to acquire the property free of debt, using the corporate assets as full security for the loan necessary to acquire the property.

You may want to require release of certain corporate assets as the principal amount of the loan is reduced.

39. Multiple Notes with One Mortgage. When you are acquiring real estate in a partnership without a down payment, the seller may be more willing to accept separate notes secured by only one mortgage on the property.

This method will provide greater flexibility if the seller plans to discount and sell the notes for cash as needed in the future.

Also, it places an obligation on the individual note signatories as members of the partnership. If one were to default, the others would be in danger of foreclosure and more likely to step in to preserve their equity.

40. Pledge Future Income as Down Payment. If you have a secure job or future investment income, negotiate with the seller to have your bank deduct a specific amount from your checking account each month until the amount the seller wanted as down payment is paid.

As additional security, give the seller a mortgage on other property to secure performance under the agreement. You get immediate ownership, and the seller eventually gets the down payment.

Chapter Seven

Institutional Financing Techniques

Knowing the loan variations possible with institutional lenders can increase the chances of getting financing. Real estate depends on credit, and when you know how to work with lenders, the chances of success increase. Any loan officer will look more favorably on someone who applies for a loan with a clear plan in hand, especially one that will make a profit for the lender with minimal risk.

Furthermore, even when what you propose is not within the power of the lender to grant, you establish a starting point for building a workable plan. Sometimes a slight change in the way your proposed financing is structured will make the deal.

Easy credit and tight money are the extremes of the lending industry. More than any other business group, lenders are at the mercy of economic cycles and monetary policy that will vary in continuing attempts to avoid deflation or inflation.

From the standpoint of an individual investor who simply wants to operate profitably within the massive unknowns of the marketplace, a few rifle shot specifics of the lending industry can help. When you know what's possible, you can choose the approach that meets your needs. When you know both what's possible and what meets your needs, you know what to ask for. New financing methods are being developed continually, especially in the area of government-backed programs. Often the solution is to ferret out that hidden government program no one else knows about.

Conventional lending policy varies throughout the country, depending on the local market and credit availability. When you are faced with a lender who is not familiar with what you propose, don't lose faith. No one can be aware of all possibilities in this fast-moving industry. Furthermore, a technique unfamiliar to your lender is not necessarily an unworkable technique. The best institutional lenders compete for loans and pride themselves on their ability to meet the needs of their customers. New technology in any industry spreads fastest when the profit motive is the driving force. Techniques used in one market can often work equally well in others, and just because they haven't been done before in one market doesn't mean they are unworkable. Lenders want to make loans that are low risk and profitable. Your job is to help them while meeting your own investment objectives. The best solutions can rise out of the process of proposing ideas that don't work, especially if the banker finds the solution after seeing your plan.

41. Wraparound Mortgage. As a *debt* investment, a wraparound mortgage is an excellent method of structuring a high yield without the usual requirement of lending the full face amount of the loan in cash. As an *equity* investment, it is a method of refinancing and cashing out the seller without paying off the current loans.

For example, an older center priced at $400,000 with $100,000 down subject to an existing $100,000 first-mortgage-bearing 7 percent interest is a likely candidate. The new first mortgage is written subject to the existing first mortgage and "wraps around" it. In some areas, this financing procedure is referred to as "all inclusive" and is set up with trust deeds.

Loan payments are made to the new lender, who is responsible for making the payments on the existing 7 percent first mortgage. The new loan has a face amount of $300,000 bearing 9 percent interest, but the new lender is required to provide only $200,000 cash. The additional $100,000 is covered by the first mortgage already on the property. Therefore, the lender collects 9 percent interest on the new $200,000 cash and an additional 2 percent interest on the $100,000 represented by the existing loan, which is $100,000 in capital the lender did not have to supply.

This approach is a solution to tight money and provides an incentive to the lender with no increase in acquisition costs. The wraparound lender is fully protected. The seller cashes out his position entirely, and the buyer is able to leverage the acquisition by establishing financing that might not otherwise be available.

42. Open End Mortgage. Under certain conditions, it is

possible to borrow back the principal paid on conventional real estate loans. This type of equity loan has grown in popularity as real estate values have increased, but can vary with credit conditions and lending policies.

The basic approach works like this. If the original loan was $150,000 and over the years it was paid down to $125,000, there is the possibility of borrowing up to the $25,000 paid and maybe more.

An open end mortgage is a source of nontaxable cash for reinvestment, for further development, or capital improvements on the property. The lender can increase the face amount of the principal and thereby increase the total dollar income from interest. There is normally a fee for this service, which is part of the incentive to do it; it can be worth the cost, provided the additional borrowings are invested in a way that creates income or appreciation.

43. Sale Buy-Back. This technique provides an additional source of profit for lenders and another incentive to provide financing. In this approach, the developer sells the land to the lending institution and immediately buys back a negotiated percentage, using a note and mortgage with release clauses. The developer gets cash from the sale that is used to develop the land, and the lender gets an equity position in the developed property that increases its profit beyond the restrictions normally imposed by a loan. It also gives the lender additional security.

This allows a developer to arrange financing in a tight credit market by providing an incentive to a lending institution through equity participation at the buyback point. The developer buys the land back using paper and takes the cash from the sale to develop the property.

44. Equity-Kicker. An equity-kicker can often mean the difference between closing a loan at a reasonable interest rate and not making the loan at all. It provides the lender with a percentage of the income generated by the property in excess of a certain amount.

For example, if the projected base income from a shopping center is $400,000 per year, the loan might stipulate that the lender will receive 15% of everything collected above $400,000. An equity-kicker may also call for a percentage of the sale price to go to the lender if the property is sold above a specified price during the first few years of the loan. A skillfully negotiated equity-kicker can attract financing in tight markets or with higher-risk projects. It gives that additional incentive often needed to complete a loan, which is a potentially higher yield.

45. REO as Incentive to Finance. Lending institutions that are burdened with REOs, or "real estate owned" (repossessed property) look more kindly toward making a loan to an investor who concurrently arranges to buy an REO.

You can look on a bank's balance sheet and see the value of the "real estate owned," which is also referred to as "other real estate owned." This property represents an undesirable asset for the lending institution because of the pressure from state banking regulations that limit the time period REOs can be carried on the books.

Repossessed property is a source of available real estate, which can often be acquired on favorable terms. It can also serve as a point of negotiation if you're trying to work out a loan by making acquisition of an unwanted REO contingent on the bank providing the financing you need.

There are many ways banks can help you reach financial objectives. The availability of REOs is another reason it pays to develop a good banking relationship. It's a source of real estate, and with the growing competition for good property, every source of potentially profitable deals should be regularly cultivated.

46. Certificate of Deposit Delivery. When a lender is reluctant to refinance property, offer to deposit a portion of the refinance proceeds in the form of a certificate of deposit. Depositing funds from a loan or opening an account with a sizable deposit can often make the difference between getting a loan and not.

Using only part of the proceeds of the refinance to acquire additional real estate is better than not raising the funds at all. Banks and savings and loans need deposits. If you can arrange deposits, chances are that your loan application will get a higher priority than that of someone who can't. The lender puts a new loan on the books and benefits by concurrently obtaining additional deposits. In times of rapid savings withdrawal, this type of incentive can make a real difference in the decision as to who gets a loan.

47. Collateral Assignment. This technique is designed to help when you negotiate a first mortgage and the lender questions your ability to repay the loan or the adequacy of the real estate you offer as security.

To solve the problem, offer to assign different property as additional security for the loan. The security is encumbered by the bank until the loan is reduced to a certain amount. The process involves a simple pledge of assets by agreement. The collateral may be other real property or personal property. Listed securities are often used.

This technique can help you obtain a loan at a higher loan-to-value ratio. In certain situations, it can increase your leverage and significantly improve your return. But as with all highly financed acquisitions, care must be taken to ensure that the investment will produce enough income to pay back the loan and show a profit. The potential reward must justify the obvious risk.

48. Negative Pledge. A negative pledge is used to protect a bank. It helps you obtain a commercial loan when the bank is relying on the condition of your financial statement at the point in time the decision is made to grant the loan.

The negative pledge differs from a regular pledge by stating that something will not be done. This contrasts with a traditional security pledge agreement, which encumbers a specific asset.

A negative pledge states that you will not encumber or dispose of any of the assets listed on your financial statement without written permission of the bank. If you violate the pledge agreement, the loan automatically becomes due. The bank is lending money based on your financial statement and the net worth it reflects at the time of the loan. Consequently, with a negative pledge, the bank is ensuring that the basis for the loan remains undisturbed. The negative pledge freezes your assets in time, and if you want to take action that may change your financial position, the bank has a chance to protect the loan. In a way, this is a method for the bank to monitor your finances over the life of the loan.

Pledging to maintain a financial statement in the condition that it was in when the bank agreed to make the loan is a small concession.

49. Letter of Credit. A letter of credit is a useful acquisition tool. Under the right conditions, it's as effective as money. It can be used as an earnest money deposit or as a down payment collectible when and if the transaction closes and the documents are recorded. It is an excellent method of tying up and acquiring real estate.

A letter of credit can fit into a variety of situations. For example, it is advantageous when a financially weak but energetic entrepreneur is backed by a financially strong investment partner or group of partners. The backer does not have to come up with cash unless the limiting conditions in the letter of credit are met. A letter of credit is usually exercisable only after a certain date and only if certain agreed events occur.

When used as earnest money it may, for instance, be exercised only after a commitment for financing is secured. If the limiting conditions of the purchase agreement are not met by a certain date, it expires automatically. The key is to never exercise the letter of credit but gain time with it to arrange financing. Attempt to mortgage out before the letter is collectible or purchase property for resale and turn it over at a profit without exercising the letter of credit used as earnest money.

For a seller, the letter of credit is protection in the event of default on the purchase agreement. When you're acquiring property with it, it is an effective method of providing earnest money consideration.

Expect to pay the bank a fee or interest for the letter of credit.

50. Compensating Balances. Many banks will lend money when they are assured of receiving compensating balances equal to the amount loaned. This allows a bank to maintain its deposit-loan ratio, and in some cases, may be the only way it can make the loan without depleting reserves. Helping lenders meet the requirements imposed by regulatory agencies and corporate policy is often the only way to get the cash you need.

It is normal practice to lend only to clients who maintain accounts with the bank providing the funds. It's virtually a prerequisite. But if money is tight, it sometimes takes even more to get the loan you need.

A solution that is quite effective involves arranging the deposit of compensating balances by a third party. Your line of credit is offset by compensating balances placed with your bank through an arrangement with another business.

Normally, the process is worked out with a company who wants your business. Title companies with large amounts of cash in transit can be helpful in this area when the end result is an increase in real estate closings for them.

51. Advance Payments Deposit. You can sometimes convince a lender of your ability to repay a loan by depositing a certain number of the monthly payments when the loan funds are disbursed. For example, your agreement might require deposit of the first year's payments at closing and the second year's payments at the beginning of the second year. You would actually be paying monthly payments in advance annually.

This technique is a way of buying time to establish credit in a new location. It's designed to demonstrate to the bank that, although your credit may not yet meet requirements, the source of loan payment funds is clearly established.

The purpose here is to offset weakness in credit history by strengthening the payback method. Keeping in mind that lenders look to credit history and a source of payback funds, this is one way of combining the two so the end result is adequate to get the loan.

52. Have Seller Move to Your Bank. Since the seller has an interest in the success of your loan, consider ways you can work with her to get the money you need to buy the property. Banks like to make loans when they get additional deposits and, in some cases, they require the checking accounts of the people to whom they lend. The seller may be more than willing to change banks if it is clear that is what it will take to sell the property.

Will it help get the loan? That depends on the size of the account and competitive stance of the bank. In growing areas, there are usually young banks in real need of new deposits. It can be a pleasure to borrow money when banks are in competitive battles. They can be quite accommodating.

If you're not working with a competitive lender, consider moving elsewhere. In any event, if you are able to attract a new (and substantial) customer to the bank as a result of buying real estate with the money you borrow, you have a distinct advantage. The bank benefits on two counts: a new loan to you, which yields a new customer for the bank.

53. Savings Account Transfer. When you are considering the transfer of business to the lender, don't overlook savings of relatives who may want to see you succeed more than they want their current bank or savings and loan association to profit. Transfer of an account can often be done without inconvenience to your helper and be timed to prevent loss of interest.

You may not think a new account is significant, but banking is becoming increasingly competitive, and loan officers earn management recognition when they bring in new business. If you help a loan officer build business, chances are he will be more inclined to help you get your loan approved.

Sizable loans must go through loan committee approval. Every person you get on your side can contribute to a favorable decision and approval of your loan request, and when you bring a new deposit with your loan application, it's one more advantage.

54. Blanket Mortgage. A blanket mortgage is one note and mortgage that encumbers two properties. It is used when the primary property borrowed against is not sufficient security for the size of the loan. Release of the additional security is normally provided when the loan is reduced to an agreed amount and should be written into the mortgage terms.

One of the requirements for obtaining any real estate loan is demonstration that there is virtually no risk for the lender. A blanket mortgage is a method of substantially eliminating risk. In many cases, it actually over-secures the loan, and that is what makes lenders happy. The additional real estate is essentially a method of making up a deficit in equity, and this is the clue to using a blanket mortgage as an acquisition method.

In the best of situations, the property used as added security will, in effect, serve as a down payment, (your equity). Consequently, the loan amount may be large enough to totally finance the new acquisition. The end result of the procedure is to provide sufficient security for the lender to make the loan. You can accomplish the same thing by selling the additional security property and making a down payment, but that would not be a wise business decision because of the tax consequences and loss of appreciation. Furthermore, it's not necessary when a blanket mortgage can be used to meet the lender's security requirements.

55. Participation. Participation is syndication of a loan involving two or more lending institutions. It spreads the risk and allows small lenders to participate in a larger loan than would have been possible otherwise. It benefits the larger institution in essentially the same way by also reducing the risk.

Generally, two banks or thrift institutions agree to provide funds when one does not have sufficient reserves to undertake the project alone. Their mutual objective, of course, is higher profits at reduced risk.

If the loan you request is too big for your bank, participation with a larger institution could help. It may require a lender from out of town. Corresponding banks in different cities have relationships designed for mutual benefit. If you live in a smaller town and have a big project, loan participation may be the solution for your plans.

56. Employer Influence. Having real trouble getting the loan? Maybe a little pressure from a major depositor such as your employer would swing the deal. This can often work smoothly with small banks when competition is rough.

This approach is the other side of providing compensating balances. Instead of bringing business to the lender, you arrange for it to keep a major depositor happy. Obviously, banks don't want to lose large accounts and normally do everything possible to make their clients happy. The exception to this general rule occurs when they are poorly managed, which does occasionally happen. In any event, a little influence from a friend or employer who is a major depositor may provide the incentive for the success of your loan application.

57. *Joint Venture.* Joint venture development projects are central to real estate and often essential as land and improvement costs escalate. The lender and developer enter into a profit-sharing partnership for development of a project such as lots in a residential subdivision. Usually the lender or its holding company will contribute partial equity in the land and provide development financing and permanent financing for the home buyers. The developer will also have an equity position in the land and handle all of the lot development engineering and preparation of the subdivision for sale to individual buyers.

Consequently, expertise and financing combine to produce a ready-to-build package for smaller builders. The joint venture group realizes the profit from lot sales and, in the process, provides an invaluable service.

Smaller builders depend on developers specializing in packaged land sales. The continuing increase in raw land costs combined with regulations for open land and environmental protection have forced all but the larger companies out of subdivision development. Joint venture projects help solve this problem and work to keep lot costs within practical limits.

58. *Long-Term Amortization with a Halfway Due Date.* This technique is used on older property or in situations where there is concern for the long-range economic stability of the area. The lender is protected by requiring full payment of the loan balance halfway through the amortization schedule (or sooner).

This may appear to be a burden but you can cut the amortization term in half by paying an amount equal to the principal due each month in addition to the regular payment. The net effect is to pay off the loan before the halfway due date by increasing the payments each month by the amount of each principal payment. Although the due date approaches fast, you do have flexibility and time to get the rents up to cover the payments without cutting into cash flow.

This type of loan is designed to accomplish another profit-oriented objective of the lender. The stated policy is to renew the loan at the halfway due date, but for a fee and at the rates in force at that time.

Therefore, the lender is not locked into an interest rate established years earlier that may be below future rates. It's also an opportunity for the lender to turn over loans more frequently and increase the net return of each loan investment. It can be a more profitable loan for the lender and a helpful refinance method for the borrower.

59. You Buy Our Stock and We'll Make Your Loan. A new bank with a stock offering that's going slowly is a lender who needs help. Offer to buy some stock if she will make your loan and thereby free up the cash you need to make the stock purchase. But do it informally so it won't be construed as a loan fee.

Again, this is one more back-scratching method. Help the lender and she'll help you. A loan officer selling stock by direction of management is usually willing to negotiate.

There are many ways to establish working relations with your bank. They boil down to getting to know helpful people. If you're serious about acquiring real estate, you must develop good banking relations. Stock ownership of a new lending institution is definitely a foot in the door.

60. Standby Commitment. If you have a good project but permanent financing is not available or is too costly, look into the possibility of a standby commitment. It will allow you to get construction financing, build the project, and if you haven't found permanent financing by then, you can exercise the standby commitment and pay off the construction loan. Commitments can run as long as three years, giving you time to find permanent financing without waiting to build and suffering the added cost of inflation in the meantime.

A standby commitment gives your construction lender the security needed to make the interim construction loan. It permits you to get the project started without delay. There's another advantage here as well. It's often easier to find permanent financing when the lender can see the project unfold. In any event, the standby commitment can be a help when money is tight but the prospects are good that money will be more readily available later.

61. Three Years with a Balloon. If you are buying property that you plan to sell within three years, this technique can increase your yield. Structure the loan for the down payment so monthly payments are low and there is a balloon when you are ready to sell. Then pay off the down payment loan with the profit from the sale.

When you structure this approach correctly, the return can be very high. You can borrow the entire amount of the down payment and then pay it off from the sale proceeds, which flow from future appreciation. The property actually buys itself. The cash flow and ultimate resale proceeds are the down payment. You simply set up the transaction so the down payment is paid out of the profit rather than out of your pocket.

62. Less than Five Years Secured. Commercial banks don't like to lend money for more than five years, and for a loan of that length, they normally want security. Knowing this in advance can help you structure your deal to meet their requirements and plan for the cash flow you need to make the deal work. The most beneficial approach is to structure the transaction so the cash flow from the property will pay off the down payment loan in five years. If you can negotiate a purchase with this in mind and then take a workable proposal to the bank, you have a head start on getting the loan.

Much of the success you have with banks depends on your loan presentation. When you're trying to borrow equity money (the down payment), thoroughness and accuracy go a long way toward soothing a loan officer's concern over risk. When the lender can see clearly that you know what you're doing, the level of risk associated with the loan drops. Approach borrowing to acquire real estate the same way you would approach borrowing for a business.

Commercial banks specialize in business loans. If you go in for a down payment loan with an income and expense history of the property and a projection of its future performance, a real estate loan begins to look more like a business loan, and that is what banks feel more comfortable with. Set up your loan request as thoroughly and accurately as you would for a business loan. Look at your personal financial statement as a company balance sheet. Structure the property history like a business profit-and-loss statement with a projection for the future. The more business-like your loan request, the more likely the response will be positive.

63. 18 Months Unsecured. If you plan to borrow on a personal note with no amortization, make the application for less than an 18-month term. This is generally the limit banks like to go on signature loans. If your signature is security enough and the short-term due date is manageable for you, this type of loan is a good source of down payment funds.

If you apply for the loan with a specific payback plan in mind, it makes it that much easier for the loan officer to approve the loan. There are two essential requirements that lenders must see in your loan request. First, there must be adequate security, which in this case is your character. Within certain limits, your signature may be security enough if you are well established in the community. Second, there must be a source of funds to repay the loan. Optimally, the income from the property will meet this requirement but a steady salary will help also.

64. The Bridge Loan. This is one application of a very helpful financing technique. When there is a time lag between two events and your funds depend on their concurrent completion, a bridge loan is a practical solution. The proceeds actually bridge the two points in time.

If you're moving out of town and don't want to wait to sell your old house before buying a new one, this might be the answer. Before you leave, arrange a short-term loan with a local bank for a portion of the equity in your house and secure it with a second mortgage. The due date should be set far enough ahead to provide enough time to sell your old house but make it due in the event the sale occurs earlier. Another approach is to borrow the down payment from a bank in the town to which you are moving, with the understanding that it will be paid when your old house sells.

For example, if the seller must close within 30 days but your financing is not available for 90 days, there is a 60-day time gap that must be covered to save the deal. A bridge loan is the way to do it.

65. Commitment Letter. If you must close an acquisition now but the mortgage rates are high and show signs of going down soon, a commitment letter may help you. First, get a letter of commitment from a savings and loan association agreeing to lend the money you need at today's rates. Then, go to a commercial bank and use the commitment letter as security to borrow the money to close. When the bank loan is due, usually six to nine months later, the rates for permanent financing may be lower. But if they're not, you can exercise the commitment and live with the higher interest.

The alternative is to let the commitment letter expire and apply for a loan at a lower rate. When a change in rates gets underway, the movement is fast regardless of the direction of the trend. Usually the turnaround points are reasonably identifiable and the trends in interest rate changes are obvious. If a change in trend indicates a lower interest cost a few months down the road, purchasing a commitment letter and setting up a short-term loan may be well worth the trouble.

Chapter Eight

Private Financing and Negotiation Techniques

One look at the variety of methods for negotiating the acquisition of real estate is enough to light a fire in the heart of any serious entrepreneur. It's also a fair test for anyone who questions the strength of his interest. There are probably as many people unnerved by unstructured opportunity as there are people who are energized by it.

People who are attracted by the virtually unlimited potential of real estate tend to do exceptionally well as they learn more of what can be done. Each new technique forms the basis for another chance to replace someone else's problem with a solution that is the basis for your opportunity.

Ultimately, it's the application of the vast body of real estate acquisition techniques that determines success, and there's no better area for applying this solution-oriented approach than in negotiating the details of a privately financed acquisition. It is what you do with the technique that makes the difference, not the technique itself.

A privately arranged acquisition that is not restricted by the mysterious reasoning of institutions or government sponsorship can take shape like a symphony. Real estate transactions are often orchestrated by artists in their fields and they are music to those who know how to hear.

Today's techniques are the starting point for what you can do. The more you know, the more you can do to expand the opportunity before you. And when you are negotiating with flexible, creative people, there's really no limit to what you can accomplish.

66. Builder's Bailout. Builders and developers who have an inventory of unsold homes can take advantage of this technique. It helps the builder out of a tight spot and can help you acquire a home without a large down payment.

You actually bail the builder out of his construction loan. This is done by making a small down payment and having the builder carry back a portion of the difference between the sale price and the new first mortgage. For example, a $150,000 home is more easily sold to someone who can buy with a minimum down payment. Under normal market conditions, the down payment is approximately 20 percent of $150,000 ($30,000). But as a sales promotion for unsold inventory, the builder may be more than willing to sell with $1,000 down to qualified buyers. You arrange a first mortgage of $120,000 and the builder carries back a second mortgage for $29,000.

This technique gives the builder an aggressive sales plan for buyers who have high incomes but not a large amount of cash. It allows a qualified buyer to purchase a home and receive the immediate benefits of ownership on good terms. Builders have been saved from bankruptcy with this approach. It provides them with relief from the interest burden of carrying the construction loan and protects their profit with the second mortgage.

67. Overpay. Overpaying the asking price is a negotiation technique designed to secure benefits that are more valuable than the price. Applying this technique requires judgment and timing during negotiations. You certainly don't want to pay more if it's not necessary. You only want to offer more if it's the only way the seller will accept your offer.

In consideration for paying more than the seller is asking, you may negotiate easier payout terms, a lower interest rate, or smaller down payment. It can also be used as a lever to obtain releases for certain portions of the real estate being acquired.

This technique is designed to provide an incentive for the seller to concede on terms she might not otherwise consider— terms that are more important to you than the price of the real estate. You can't meet your profit objectives if you don't acquire the real estate. This technique is an effective method of making sure you get the property. The seller may be motivated when she realizes more total profit from the sale than originally anticipated or even requested.

68. Contingent Price Sale. A contingent price sale is an acquisition at a value to be determined by the future performance of the property. The sales price is set as a function of the income produced by the property.

When you suspect hidden problems with a property, this technique can make the difference between a successful acquisition and a failure. There are a number of ways to structure the payout details. Generally, though, you could capitalize the operating income over a given time period to establish the total sales price. Although the seller may require a minimum base, you can establish the maximum total price by dividing the annual income by the return you want. For example, a net operating income before debt service of $50,000 divided by 10 percent results in a price of $500,000. If the income is $45,000 the sales price drops to $450,000 for a 10 percent return. This is just one way of many to structure a contingent price sale. A variation in the price formula may be necessary to account for financing.

Another application is to avoid a base sales price and simply agree to pay the seller a specified percentage of the profits over a limited time period. If you are involved in a contingent price sale, be sure to investigate the tax advantages to the seller. With proper tax counsel, the seller may find the tax advantage worth the risk of a contingent price.

69. Private Wraparound. One of the most beneficial ways for a seller to carry an equity balance is a wraparound mortgage. This can be structured by using a number of different instruments, such as a mortgage, trust deed, or real estate contract. The particular document used can best be determined by state law. The financial benefits will be the same.

The procedure is simple. The seller receives a first lien position subject to the existing loan, which is paid monthly out of the buyer's payments on the new wraparound. The seller gets interest on the dollar balance of his equity, plus additional interest on the difference between the existing loan rate and the higher interest on the wraparound.

This is an excellent method for a seller and can offer an incentive for other concessions when negotiating an acquisition. If the existing loan is $80,000 at 8 percent interest and the seller agrees to a wraparound mortgage at 9 percent, here's how it would work. With a sales price of $160,000 and $20,000 cash down payment, the seller's equity balance is $60,000. But the face value of the wraparound mortgage is $140,000. Consequently, the seller receives interest of 9 percent on his equity of $60,000 and an additional one percent on the underlying 8 percent mortgage of $80,000. This can be quite an incentive for a seller who understands compound interest.

70. Seller as Short-Term Lender. This is a method of working with the seller to avoid high interest rates. If the seller wants terms that require refinancing but interest rates are too high, this approach may solve the problem.

Negotiate with the seller to carry the amount that would have been paid off by refinancing. Then set a due date a couple of years away or sooner if you obtain a satisfactory loan rate.

This will allow you to close the transaction now and give you the chance to set up permanent financing at a lower cost as interest rates drop.

71. Vary the Loan Payments Based on Occupancy. This technique ties the payments on a purchase money mortgage directly to the occupancy of the acquired property.

For example, if you're acquiring a 20-unit apartment complex with a questionable future, structure the financing with the seller so that if the occupancy rate is 90 percent, the interest rate on the carry-back loan stays at 9 percent. But if occupancy drops to 80 percent, the interest rate drops to 8 percent. The reduction would continue at a ratio of a one percent drop in interest for each 10 percent drop in occupancy.

There are a couple of variations to this approach that can be helpful. If occupancy drops below a certain rate, you might want a temporary suspension in amortization of loan principal and pay only the interest until things improve. Another variation is to decrease the total amount of the loan payment rather than just the interest. In some cases where the loans provide for a large monthly amortization of principal, it may not be necessary to decrease the amount of interest paid at all. The object is to decrease monthly debt service to avoid a negative cash flow. Whether you whittle the interest or principal portion of the payment depends on what the seller can live with.

72. Improvement Costs as Return of Down Payment. If you are acquiring property that needs repair and is a questionable investment due to its present condition, consider negotiating with the seller to put the cash that would normally go to the down payment into repairs. You can protect your position and the seller by setting up the purchase to upgrade the property.

It's not unusual for property to be sold because the owner is unable or unwilling to spend the money necessary to bring it up to market potential. Furthermore, it may be necessary to put a certain amount of money into the property just to protect it. By agreeing with the seller to divert the down payment to repairs, you will give him better protection on the equity he carries on a purchase money mortgage.

Consequently, you can acquire real estate in a condition that ensures a profitable operation. The seller gets the full purchase price in the form of the purchase money mortgage, and you get your cash outlay (that would have gone to the seller) back in property value.

Putting the down payment into the improvements may be necessary to ensure a profitable operation and timely payment of the seller's carry-back mortgage, but there's another benefit as well. If the seller insists on cash, there's a possibility he may get more in the long run if the improvements are sufficient to permit refinancing. This would of course cash out the seller and may increase his willingness to take the deal.

73. Moratorium on Debt Service. If you are acquiring a one-tenant building and there is a question as to whether the lease will be renewed, some degree of protection can be ensured by negotiating a stop to the loan payments if the building becomes vacant. Usually you will have to put a time limit on the moratorium, with the understanding that the purpose is to give you enough breathing room to find a new tenant. Three to six months is a good starting point.

By including this relatively minor provision in a purchase money mortgage, you may avoid a serious problem in the future.

128

The objective is to lessen the risk of acquiring income property that depends on the continued occupancy of one tenant. A warehouse acquisition is a likely candidate for protection using this formula.

74. Automatic Discount. An automatic discount should always be part of your acquisition strategy. When you're acquiring property with a substantial purchase money mortgage and there's a possibility of refinancing it in the future, this technique can mean real savings.

For example, a $100,000 carry-back mortgage on a $150,000 purchase might provide for an automatic discount of 10 percent (about $10,000) if paid in full within two years. The objective of the seller is to provide an incentive for the buyer to cash him out. Consequently, a drop in the discount after two years to 5 percent is an appropriate extension of the technique. Of course, when you're acquiring the property and paying on the note, you want the longest time possible at the maximum discount the seller will accept.

This technique allows you to reduce the total sales price by transferring the bargaining point from the property to the note and mortgage. The possibility of a future cash-out can be an incentive for a seller to reduce the sales price, and negotiating it into the future gives you breathing room to refinance. Even if it proves impossible to take advantage of, you lose nothing by setting it up. There's always the possibility you will sell the property during the discount period to a cash buyer and then the importance of the discount will be measurable.

75. Interest Only Until the First Is Paid. By negotiating an interest only payment until the existing first mortgage is paid, you can minimize the drain on the cash flow from debt service. This technique is especially helpful when the seller is asking a high price and you want to maximize the tax shelter aspects of the property.

There are two major benefits to this technique: an increase in your cash flow because you are not paying off the principal balance of the purchase money mortgage and a more efficient use of the available tax deductions because the interest payment is deductible.

This technique is a way of maximizing your cash flow in any situation, but in some cases, it is essential to the profitability of the acquisition. You are asking the seller to defer payment of the equity represented by the purchase money mortgage. And from a time value standpoint, that is money in your pocket today and more valuable than it would have been if you had received it in the future.

When the cash flow is questionable, this approach helps offset the risk. It's one more tool that can be combined with the other techniques to minimize your risk and maximize your profit.

76. Balloon Payments. Structuring private financing with well-timed balloon payments can often mean the difference between completing a transaction and letting it die from lack of ingenuity. A balloon payment is a lump sum principal payment that comes at the maturity of a note. But balloon payments can be placed at various points throughout a loan to provide an incentive for the seller to accept a smaller down payment or other terms you may want.

One clever application is the holiday season balloon, which calls for an additional lump sum payment each year during the first part of December. The strategy is to give the seller an incentive to offset other terms of the acquisition that are more important to you.

Periodic balloon payments in addition to the regular amortization payments can often lower the amount of down payment required by the seller. Knowing he will receive beneficially timed balloon payments can be more important than a large one-time down payment. The first part of April is another helpful date to receive cash because of income taxes.

The other benefit from balloon payments is that they can be used to structure an installment sale. Rather than lose the important benefits of installment reporting, it is much wiser to spread a down payment over a couple of years in the form of a balloon payment.

When you are acquiring real estate, balloon payments can help defer an immediate cash outlay for the down payment. But the way you time the payments will provide the incentive for the seller.

77. Sell with Option to Buy Back. If you're having difficulty getting a seller to part with his property, offer him an option to buy it back. This can be a form of protection for someone who thinks he may be selling too soon, and it's a small concession for you when the alternative is no transaction at all.

The terms of the buy-back option can be flexible. You should build in a reasonable profit in case the seller does exercise the option. The danger is that the seller has a marketable right in the option and may choose to sell the option itself to someone who wants to exercise it. To prevent this, you can negotiate a clause that makes the option nontransferable.

This approach has been used successfully in joint ventures with options to buy partial ownership. In one case, an investor retained an option to acquire a 25 percent ownership position in an office building developed on his land. The option had a five-year life and was eventually sold for a substantial profit when an insurance company bought the entire project.

There are several ways this technique can be worked into the specific requirements of any transaction. It's an aid to acquiring property when the seller wants to have his cake and eat it too. But it's also a financing tool for a seller who wants to raise money by selling now while still retaining the possibility of participating in future profits.

78. Reduce the Interest but Increase the Monthly Payment. When you are negotiating private financing, the major objective is to retain as many benefits as possible, whether you are buying or selling. One way of structuring the benefits is to vary the components of the monthly payment. A portion of the monthly payment goes to interest and the remainder reduces the loan balance.

This technique uses the monthly payment to satisfy the seller's desire for rapid payoff. Instead of a balloon payment, you reduce the interest but increase the amount of the monthly loan payment, and consequently, the principal portion of the payment. The net effect is an increase in the speed with which the seller receives the total sales price.

It will also increase the amount of the loan payment allocated at lower capital gains tax rates for the seller. When you use this technique, you benefit by paying less interest and therefore fewer total dollars (interest plus principal) over the life of the mortgage. Of course, you will have less monthly cash flow and a smaller interest deduction.

79. Reduce the Monthly Payment but Increase the Interest. Another method of using debt service payments to your advantage is to reduce the monthly payment but increase the interest. If the seller wants long-term income, increase the interest rate and maintain a low portion of the loan payment for principal reduction. This will stretch out the term of the loan and give the seller a large dollar amount of ordinary income from interest. It will also increase the total cost of the property acquisition, but your annual net tax deduction will be larger due to the increased interest.

The point here is to meet the seller's requirements without destroying the profitability of the property. This approach allows the seller to maintain the amount of the debt investment (loan principal balance) and receive income from it in the form of interest over a longer period. A tradeoff for stretching out the amortization is the increase in net cash flow of the property as a result of a smaller debt service payment.

80. Sale Lease-Back. A sale lease-back is one of the more effective real-estate acquisition methods. It is frequently used by large businesses but it can be equally beneficial for any size transaction when the seller is financially strong and wants to continue using the property.

This technique builds income into the transaction. Essentially, the seller agrees to sell and lease back at a rental rate based on the sales value of the property. This establishes a rate of return without the usual concern about finding tenants.

A sale lease-back is often used when an owner wishes to raise cash without losing use of the real estate. The objective in this application is to obtain capital for the business to finance expansion. If a corporation is in a growth industry, why tie up capital by owning real estate? The business will make more money by concentrating on its specialty rather than the ownership of real estate. Consequently, a sale lease-back can often be viewed as a financing method from the seller's point-of-view.

Acquiring property that is leased back by the seller can give you quite an advantage. With a financially strong seller signing the lease, it's possible to obtain 100 percent financing. Of course, the details of sales price, interest rates, and lease terms play an important role in the potential profit.

81. Add the Interest to Principal. Property that does not have adequate cash flow to cover the debt service of a second mortgage is an opportunity for payment of interest only with no amortization of the second mortgage principal. In extreme cash flow problems, part of the interest not covered by income can be added to the loan principal. This is a temporary solution to the negative cash flow created by over financing or inadequate rental income and a limited-time measure designed to give you an opportunity to increase the income on the property.

Not all property starts out making money, and if you're acquiring property that won't cover the debt service required by the second mortgage, this technique is a way to buy time. As the interest increases, the loan principal compounds rapidly, raising the amount of indebtedness on the property. But in some cases, it only takes a little time and remodeling to turn property around.

This technique allows you to negotiate a loan that is designed to meet the seller's requirements and the limitations of the existing cash flow on the property. It provides time to set up your turnaround program and make the property productive.

The objective is to build the income up enough to amortize the loan principal. Although it is a somewhat undesirable position to be in, there are benefits. The seller gets the added compounding value of interest paid on interest. And it increases the total dollar return he will get for the property while compensating him for the delay.

82. Three-Year Interest-Only Balloon. A three-year interest only payment followed by a balloon for the total amount of the mortgage can be a helpful way to structure the acquisition of vacant land. If you sell within the three-year period, the return will be higher because of the minimum paid for amortization of debt.

The objective is to resell the property prior to the balloon. The funds for payment of the balloon come from the new buyer's financing. In the event the property is not sold, you have ample time to locate financing to pay the balloon as it comes due. This is a logical opportunity to negotiate a discount as part of the mortgage if you make the balloon payment early. It's a natural for an automatic discount.

The all-cash payoff at the end of three years is the incentive for the seller to accept interest only. It may hit that middle ground between all cash at closing and a long payout that meets your needs and the seller's.

83. Subordination to Construction Financing. If you are ready to build but don't have the cash necessary to pay off the existing land loan, subordination is one solution. The holder of the existing financing agrees to subordinate his security position to a new construction loan. When building is complete and permanent financing is established, the existing loan is paid in full. Consequently, there is a period of increased risk for the existing note holder because, if there is a default, the construction lender will have first claim to the property.

Also, if you're planning to acquire vacant land for development and want to maximize leverage, negotiate subordination of the seller's interest to construction financing as part of the purchase. This will allow you to build without paying off the land until construction is complete and the permanent financing is in force. This approach works to maximum benefit when combined with a mortgage-out strategy.

84. Subordination for Cash. If you own property that can be refinanced, ask the holder of the first mortgage to subordinate his mortgage to a new first mortgage. As an incentive, you might agree to pay an extra amount on your existing loan. With that unexpected cash incentive, the first mortgage holder may be willing to accept a secondary position, thus giving you the opportunity to pull out tax-free cash for acquisition of more real estate.

Subordination of a first lien position is normally associated with development, but it can also be a successful method of raising cash for acquisition. Vacant land that is encumbered and ready for development is the usual candidate for a subordination agreement, but it can be equally effective when you want to raise acquisition capital, whether your property is improved or vacant land. The only requirement is that it can be refinanced. The problem is convincing the note holder to take a subordinate lien position, because it increases risk.

Therefore, to offset the increase in risk, an additional cash payment is made. Ideally, this payment will reduce the existing loan. In difficult situations, it may be necessary (and profitable) to pay an added cash bonus over and above the loan amount. It can be well worth paying a little extra when the end result is tax-free cash in your account. If the economics of the property support the new loan, the note holder may be in a better financial position than before.

85. Purchase Money Mortgage. This popular approach is often used when the seller wants installment reporting or when institutional financing is not available. The seller deeds to the buyer, and the buyer gives a note secured by a mortgage to the seller. The seller consequently has a first mortgage position secured by the property he sold. In the event of default, the seller would foreclose. This is a private adaptation of standard institutional financing without the transfer of lump sum financing. The seller gets his money as the payments are made.

It is really a form of documentation, as are so many techniques. Often both buyer and seller know where they want to end up, and the only requirement is setting up the paperwork to get there. That's one reason why it's important to know the possible techniques; then you can explore alternatives with the seller during negotiation. It's the exploration process that touches the new alternatives that may be entirely acceptable to the seller. How many real estate transactions do you suppose have failed simply because the people involved didn't have access to the alternative that would get the job done? How many are stopped in their tracks because when the solution appeared they accepted someone's offhand remark of "impossible" or "that won't work"?

86. Real Estate Contract. Sometimes called a sales contract, land sales contract, or contract of sale, this approach to private financing provides a practical solution to the problem of foreclosure. The buyer contracts with the seller to purchase real estate. The real estate contract and the deed conveying title to the buyer are held in escrow until the terms of the contract are met, then the deed is recorded. A special deed is also placed in escrow deeding the property from the buyer back to the seller. This deed is recorded only if the buyer defaults under the terms of the contract. This eliminates the lengthy foreclosure process. It's also final. There is no redemption.

Real estate contracts are usually set up as standard printed forms in states where they are commonly used. The terms and details of the document vary in different localities, depending on state law.

The benefit of the real estate contract is the flexibility it provides for the buyer and seller to establish terms that meet their mutual objectives. It can be especially useful when you assume the existing mortgage and the seller accepts a down payment that doesn't cash out the entire equity. The real estate contract makes up the difference. Its face value is the seller's remaining equity. When the contract is paid in full, usually by monthly payments, the escrow company releases the deed for recording.

87. Second Mortgage or Second Trust Deed. When a buyer assumes an existing loan, the seller will often be forced by reasonableness to carry back a portion of the equity on a second mortgage or trust deed. With this approach to private financing, you get a deed to the property subject to the existing loan. Rather than sign a contract that must be performed, you sign a promissory note secured by a second mortgage.

In some states, a trust deed is used instead of a mortgage. There are legal differences from state to state, but for our purposes, the important factor is the negotiation possibilities of the documentation.

One element any buyer should pay close attention to is the extent of personal liability possible in the event of default. As real estate prices explode beyond reasonable measures of value, there are certain considerations that should be kept in mind when signing notes for real estate acquisitions.

In the event the bottom drops out of the economy and you lose your real estate, what happens under the terms of the note and mortgage you sign? If you paid more for the property when you acquired it than it's worth under the depressed market condition in force when you lost it, there can be a negative consequence. If it can't be sold for enough to pay off the note you signed, the mortgage holder can sue you for the deficiency, which is the difference between the lower market price and the amount you owe. If the court rules against you, a deficiency judgment is handed down, requiring you to pay the deficiency. If you don't, your other personal assets can be attached and sold. This is one good reason not to be caught in excessive speculation. It is possible to lose more than the property itself if you are not careful.

Any good real estate financing technique can be used imprudently, but don't let it happen to you. If you are acquiring property that has even the remotest possibility of ending up in trouble, insist on a limit to personal liability on the note you sign. None is a good start.

88. Pledge, Collateralize, or Hypothecate. Using additional collateral is often a help in closing an acquisition, especially when the down payment is less than the seller feels is necessary for security against default. Insurance cash value, stocks, bonds, personal property, or other real estate all serve the purpose.

If the seller feels she needs a 20 percent down payment but you have only 10 percent, take a close look at other assets you own. Determine what the seller is trying to accomplish by requiring a 20 percent down payment. Security is more than cash. If the seller is willing to wait for cash, hypothecating anything of value may provide sufficient security.

The key is searching out what the seller wants. That's why it can be crucial for someone involved in the negotiations to know what the seller wants to accomplish and what is necessary to accomplish it. It may well be that the primary objective is to get out of management headaches, and a no down payment sale to an effective manager would be more satisfactory than 20 percent down by someone who will ruin the property and default on the mortgage.

89. Private Insurance Annuity. An income for life can be more appealing to a seller than a sale. One way to provide income is to purchase an annuity from an insurance company that will continue for the life of the seller. The seller deeds the real estate to you free and clear and receives an income for life. The property is refinanced to generate the cash necessary to buy the annuity.

Another approach to acquisition by annuity is used between relatives. It has greater flexibility and does not involve the outright purchase of an annuity. An annuity agreement is used which establishes the payment terms. It simply states that payment for life will be provided as consideration for the property.

In this case, the seller relies only on the private agreement for future income. That's why it's generally more appropriate for use with relatives. There's no reason for this unfunded approach not to be used between individuals who are not related if the necessary trust and asset base are there.

The obvious benefit is what you can do with free-and-clear income-producing property if you don't have to borrow against it to purchase the annuity. It can serve as the basis for building an investment portfolio and provide the income to pay the annuity.

90. Purchase a Remainder Interest. In some situations, the only way a seller will part with property is by retaining use of it during the balance of her lifetime. You can accomplish this by purchasing a remainder interest in the property and allowing the seller to retain a life estate interest. The seller gets all income from the property until death, plus the cash and notes you pay at closing.

This technique may be combined with a management agreement permitting you to operate the property to protect your interests. On the death of the seller, the entire fee interest automatically transfers to you.

Purchasing a remainder interest is an example of how a transaction can be closed even when the timing is not exactly right. It's a solution for what may seem an insurmountable barrier. It is also potentially beneficial for the seller. The cash from a sale now may be much more useful.

Since you're not receiving income during the balance of the seller's life, there is a certain price adjustment that can be made to compensate. This may be offset by calculation of the property appreciation factor, which may be required in determining the remainder interest.

91. Walk the Mortgage. This technique has many applications. Walking the mortgage is a process of substituting different real estate as security for an existing mortgage. The mortgage is modified or rewritten to encumber different real estate. The objective is to free up property that can be easily refinanced. This technique can provide significant future benefits if you negotiate it into the terms of property you're acquiring. Even if it isn't agreed to in advance by the seller, it's an excellent method of maximizing refinance proceeds if you can negotiate it later.

The significant factor is the flexibility that walking the mortgage gives you. It allows you to free up equity. Equity is acquisition power. This technique really hits home when you use it to refinance appreciated property.

In one case, an investor was able to walk a $45,000 mortgage from a fourplex to a large tract of vacant land. Although the land was good security, banks wouldn't lend on it. But the individual who held the purchase money mortgage on the fourplex was happy to cooperate, especially after receiving a reasonable cash incentive.

92. Reversing the Interest. By structuring an acquisition with separate notes that are due annually, you can place the high interest payments at the end of the amortization term rather than at the beginning. Negotiate the transaction so that each note is paid, plus accrued interest, at the end of every 12 months. For example, the first note bears one year's interest, the fifth bears five years' interest, and the twentieth bears 20 years' interest. Each year has a separate note. It may take 20 years of $10,000 notes to pay off the property. One mortgage is used to secure all the notes.

This technique intentionally places the burden of making large payments in the later years. It also gives you a larger deduction toward the end of the amortization term. The seller can defer ordinary income in the earlier years of the sale because the interest is reversed. This approach can be of benefit to someone who is retiring and anticipates being in a lower tax bracket as time passes. Consequently, it would be advantageous to take a greater portion of capital gains now and defer receipt of the higher-taxed interest income. Be careful with this one. Compound interest grows fast.

93. This Year's Interest as Down Payment. The use of several years' prepaid interest as down payment has been eliminated from the beneficial tax techniques available to purchasers. This advanced deduction was a help with taxes and can still be used to some degree as a negotiating advantage when you are purchasing property at the beginning of the tax year.

If you are buying with virtually all paper and little cash, offer to pay the balance of the year's interest in advance in lieu of a cash down payment. This may give the seller the cash necessary to put his mind at ease. It will also increase the effective yield on the carry back paper. When used in conjunction with an interest-only mortgage, it results in acquisition with fully deductible dollars.

The most advantageous acquisition methods are those that do not require use of your own cash. When you can't quite reach this ideal objective, the next best approach is to maximize the deductibility of the cash you do put into the acquisition.

Often a down payment requirement is half need and half greed. If you can negotiate out the greed part and make the balance tax deductible interest, it's a big step toward maximizing profit.

94. The Bargain Sale. The bargain sale is a method of reducing the sales price for a nonprofit organization. It is often used in the sale of land for the location of a school or church when the owner of the land has a connection with the nonprofit organization and wants to make a tax-deductible donation.

The price of the property is established by appraisal. A sales agreement is then signed that divides the price between the donated amount and cash. For example, the property owner might agree to donate 90 percent of the appraised value and sell 10 percent for cash. This creates a significant bargain for the nonprofit and a substantial deduction for the property owner.

A million dollar property would reflect a $900,000 donation, which has a cash value in tax savings of $315,000 for someone with a 35 percent effective tax bracket (0.35 x 900,000 = 315,000). When this amount is added to the 10 percent cash payment, it results in cash of $415,000 for the property.

For high-income owners, this is a natural method of helping a nonprofit while realizing partial cash for the property. And it facilitates a true bargain for the nonprofit.

95. The Diamonds Down Payment. Diamonds of investment quality tend to increase in value during inflationary cycles. However, diamonds are not easy to sell. The ready market is the wholesale market, and you need to know your merchandise to compete with other sellers. This is one asset you always want to buy at the wholesale price from a reputable dealer.

But if you have a diamond with a good written appraisal, it can make a useful down payment. Instead of paying cash as a down payment, consider using an appraised diamond ring. Given the lack of liquidity of diamonds on the open market, you can increase the marketability of the asset by transferring it to real estate equity. This requires some negotiation, but keep in mind that the right commission for a real estate broker may be a nice ring or two. And diamonds can go a long way toward meeting the down payment requirement, if not cover it entirely.

96. Lower the Interest and Increase the Price. This method decreases the ordinary income to the seller from interest but makes up the difference in capital gain from the sale. The seller's aftertax income is increased through the benefits of capital gains without causing him to sacrifice the total cash in his pocket.

If you don't mind losing an interest deduction, this technique can have an impact on the success of the acquisition when there's competition for property. First, get the seller's attention by offering more for the property. Then, explain how the low interest and high price adjustment will convert a large portion of the combined sales proceeds (interest and principal) to lower capital gains rates.

The key is to calculate the total dollars you would pay for the property at a certain high interest rate. Then calculate the total at a much lower rate. Add part of the difference to the seller's price. The seller pays more of the price at a lower capital gains rate and gets more net aftertax income. Although you lose an interest deduction, it may be a small price to pay when competition for property is rough and the alternative is not closing the deal.

97. Management Fee for Specific Services. If the seller is going to be involved in the management of the property after the sale, this technique can help reduce your net cost by structuring part of the offer as payment for management services.

141

This is another way of building a deductible payment into the acquisition. Management fees for specific services after you acquire the property are deductible operating expenses.

If you're involved in negotiations that appear to be headed toward free management provided by the seller, consider paying for it and reducing the purchase price. The total dollars received by the seller will be unchanged, but you will have an additional deduction. Furthermore, structuring the transaction this way will more accurately reflect payment for what you receive.

98. Applying the Multiparty Exchange as an Acquisition Technique. Structuring an exchange can be the solution to the problem of an owner who is reluctant to sell when discovering the impact of capital gains tax on the transaction.

Applying the benefits of exchanging as a help in an acquisition strategy is fundamental to the multiparty exchange. It is popular in part because it facilitates the acquisition of real estate that has a large profit that would be lost to taxes in an outright sale.

Exchanging is the solution to the tax problems of highly appreciated property. Conversely, exchanging is also the solution for the buyer who is confronted with an owner who refuses to sell because of the tax consequences. For the owner, it is the only method of disposing of the property that is acceptable. Consequently, for the buyer, it is the only method of acquiring the property that will work.

A strong desire to acquire a specific investment property is a major reason the multiparty exchange exists today. It is primarily an acquisition technique. A buyer wants to acquire a property that can't be sold because of the tax consequences; therefore, the owner finds other property, which the buyer acquires and exchanges for the owner's original property without tax consequences. The application of the multiparty exchange as a solution to the tax problems encountered when trying to acquire real estate places it at the head of the list of techniques to use when you want a specific property and the seller does not want to pay tax on the disposition.

Chapter Nine

Using a Lease to Acquire Real Estate

Land may be the backbone of real estate, but leasing is the muscle. Real estate starts with land and becomes a business with a lease. Land is a store of value. Leasing is a method of extracting the stored value.

It's the use of real estate that produces income. By definition, when you're working with the leasing process you're involved in the use of real estate for the production of income. From an investment standpoint, it is often the structure of the lease that establishes the profit potential.

Shopping centers have become sought-after investments, largely due to the accepted practice of tying a lease to the gross sales of the tenant. A percentage lease assures the center owner of a growing income as the tenant's business prospers. Often the tenant succeeds only because of the drawing power of the shopping center and profits far more than would be possible in a relatively isolated location.

Triple net or absolute net leases have demonstrated investment benefits of a different kind. If you're after management-free ownership, they're the answer. Often used with the sale leaseback of single-use buildings, they provide reasonable returns without the problems of management.

Leasing can play an important role in your acquisition plans. It ties directly to financing as proof of income to service debt. In fact, when you look for acquisition financing and have a lease in hand, you're practically in business.

99. Bond Lease. One of the most reliable, often-used methods to acquire real estate with a minimum of cash starts with the bond lease. This technique requires a tenant with a high credit rating who is willing to sign a long-term lease. The best candidates are national tenants with high performance ratings.

The basic process involves using the lease commitment to secure financing. Whether you're building a new building or buying an existing one, the commitment to lease is the first step. The lease is security for the financing and in effect guarantees repayment of the loan.

Usually, the lender requires that the term of the lease equal or exceed the time required to amortize the loan. This approach can also be used with smaller individual companies with good credit ratings.

Using a bond lease to acquire real estate has an obvious and immediate benefit: you start with a reliable tenant. This fact opens the door to financing and, when you have both good income and financing, you're well on the way to a profitable transaction. The key is putting all the components together so the net result is positive cash flow.

100. Lease-Condo. This technique is designed as an incentive to potential tenants for professional office space that is difficult to lease. It can form the basis for acquisition of property no one else can deal with. The decision to buy real estate is easier when you see a way to make a profit that others have overlooked.

Offer current tenants and prospective new tenants space for a certain period of time, say four years. In your proposal, agree to apply part of the lease payment as credit toward purchase of the space leased. Structure the lease so the tenant will have accumulated enough credit toward the down payment to make the purchase without additional cost.

This is an incentive for the tenant to set up business in a building that may not be in the most desirable location. It is also a solution for an owner who is having difficulty leasing. It is certainly better than having a building that can't be sold as an investment sit vacant.

There are certain important requirements that must be planned into the project. Conversion to condominium space has become widespread and a common practice in many areas, so the mechanics are somewhat routine. Since you're dividing the ownership, you will need to have the individual spaces surveyed to establish legal descriptions. Individual financing will be necessary for each professional office.

101. Sandwich Lease. A sandwich lease is an excellent method of controlling property and generating investment income without capital. The key is to lease property that can be re-leased at a higher rate. Your lease is then sandwiched between the owner and the new tenant, who pays a higher rent to you than you pay to the property owner.

You can use a number of methods to get the initial lease at a lower rate. If the market is depressed, maybe the owner would be happy to lease it at a rent less than you calculate the market will be after the slump turns to a recovery. If the property needs work, agree to upgrade it if the owner will give you a long-term lease at a low rate.

Negotiating the economics is the key, but in any event you should plan to include an option to purchase as part of the lease. This can be an important part of the strategy, especially if the market improves.

By signing a lease when the market is depressed and putting personal effort into upgrading the property, you may see a drastic increase in its value when rental conditions improve. Furthermore, when you lease at a higher rate, the property value automatically increases based on an income approach to appraisal. Its investment attractiveness will improve and, with an option to purchase at the previous value, the profit will be yours.

102. Master Lease as Security for Development. A master lease is an overriding lease of a building (usually an office or shopping complex). It is used to guarantee a return to the owner in a sale-leaseback transaction or, in some cases, to secure permanent financing. The developer of a project may underwrite sale of the project to a limited partnership and concurrently provide security for the long-term lender by establishing a master lease. The signatory to the master lease then covers the obligation by leasing to individual tenants.

In a way, the master lease is an insurance policy against loss of rent. Its purpose is to establish a base return on investment for the owner and, in some cases, a guarantee for payment of debt service during the rent-up phase of a new development.

When you are acquiring property with a strong master lease

signed by someone who knows what he's doing or a company with strong management and financial capabilities, it simply reduces the risk. It also increases your ability to obtain financing. Be careful, though. If the property itself is headed for trouble, you may be forced to depend on the party signing the master lease. Of course, this is the purpose of the master lease, but when things don't work out as planned, even the strongest companies try to renegotiate.

103. Management Lease-back. This approach is often used in the sale of apartments to a limited partnership. A management company, which is more than likely a subsidiary of the company selling the limited partnership units, will lease the entire property after the sale. The limited partnership, therefore, has no concern over management, and the sales organization has a built-in aid. By arranging the lease-back concurrently with the offering, the investors know what their return will be and will be more willing to invest.

This is an application of the master lease designed to meet the needs of investors who must be satisfied with both the professional management and projected return before committing funds. It takes the risk down to a minimal level.

Real estate companies that specialize in limited partnership offerings are practically required to provide management for the property they sell. Often they have a separate corporation staffed by professional managers that handles this. A management leaseback actually transfers economic risk from the investors to the management company. The company is compensated for this risk by the income produced in excess of the leaseback obligation.

Consequently, negotiation of the master lease must take the normal management fee and the risk premium into consideration. The result is more income for the company and less risk for the investors.

104. Lease Back the Vacancies. If you are acquiring property that has a high vacancy rate, ask the owner to lease the vacant units for a certain period of time to ensure your return. The seller only has to lease enough units to bring the cash flow up to a reasonable return. This approach avoids the extensive liability of a master lease-back and provides a method of reducing the seller's obligation as the vacant units are rented to new tenants.

Leasing back the vacancies is one of the many ways of working around apparent problems to structure a successful closing. If you are acquiring property with vacancies that exceed the risk you are willing to take, this technique may help.

Sellers who are tired of management and willing to work with you to solve their problems by helping you meet your objectives will often share risk to ensure a sale. If the transaction is on the borderline between problems and profit and you need that little incentive to go ahead, offsetting the vacancies can turn a questionable deal into a positive venture.

105. Lease Cash-Out. If you are acquiring land that has potential for a lease, locate a tenant at the same time you make the purchase. Then take the lease to a lender as security in addition to the land itself and borrow the money to acquire the land. Income from the lease will offset the loan payments, and the land seller will cash out, possibly at a price favorable to you.

This technique converts a potential passive land investment into a business opportunity. Any time you can change the earnings performance of property concurrently with acquisition you tend to increase value. When you enter an acquisition that involves making raw land income producing, you move considerably closer to a business.

Arranging a lease for the land you want is like creating the money needed to make the purchase. The future income represented by the lease has a present value. If that present value equals your purchase price, chances are you can acquire the land with no cash out of pocket.

The seller's cooperation will be essential and there is good reason to help out. When you finish putting the pieces together, the seller will cash out. As you proceed, be sure to make the steps interdependent. Make the purchase contingent on financing and finalizing a land lease. Offer to cash out the seller only if every part of the transaction fits together as planned.

106. Land Sale Lease-Back for Development. By selling and leasing back commercial land, it is possible to raise the cash necessary to complete development. Construction costs sometimes exceed the funds available for building. Consequently, a developer may have to sell part or all of the project land to raise development funds.

For example, it may be possible to raise sufficient cash by selling the parking area to an investor and leasing back. The land investor's interest would be subject to construction and permanent financing. The transaction adds cash to cover construction and complete the project.

Selling property and leasing it back is a common financing technique. Applying this method to parking areas and freestanding portions of a shopping center such as automobile repair centers simplifies the requirements. In fact, if you anticipate the possibility of needing additional funds, try to hold back these somewhat separate land areas from your construction mortgage. This will avoid having to negotiate a partial release to structure a land sale lease-back later.

107. Package the Leases and Sell Out. This approach is designed to affect a rapid turnover of capital by packaging the entire project, including lease commitments, financing, city approvals grading and drainage plans, and the construction contract. Virtually all of this is done on paper, with a relatively minimal out-of-pocket expense. The cash comes when the package is sold to an investor at a profit. The cash outlay by the investor covers the real estate equity requirement and the value created by putting the package together. The investor gets a fully organized project and none of the headaches of putting it together. This approach is sometimes the first step for establishing a limited partnership of investors, which spreads the risk.

It takes skill and hard work to set up a successful shopping center or office development. In the short run, getting tenants signed on leases is as valuable as land ownership is over the long run. The value created by the lease commitments is saleable. Selling a complete project package is a way of pulling out the value created by the initial development efforts. It's a quick turnover of the capital used to put the deal together without the wait normally associated with long-term real estate investment.

With the steady growth in city requirements and regulations, both the value and the cost of packaging a development project are increasing. As a business segment of the real estate industry, it has potential.

108. Lease When You Can't Buy. If you have spent time trying to acquire land, no doubt you have run into owners who refuse to sell but will lease. Although it is frustrating, the wisdom of their plan is apparent. Even in this situation there are advantages.

Leasing land eliminates the need for large amounts of front-end capital. Furthermore, if you plan to build and the landowner agrees to subordinate her interest to financing, the possibility that you will be able to mortgage out increases. You will be able to put the deal together with less cash since you don't have to buy the land. By leasing land, you gain control. What you do with that control will determine your profit. In that sense, it's no different than outright ownership.

The extent of the long-term success with a land lease depends to a large degree on what you can include and keep out of the original lease terms. Try to include an option to buy. Work toward an option that can be exercised after a reasonable time. In any event, push to get an option even if it's exercisable in 50 years or only after the death of the owner's last child.

It's crucial to avoid imprudent and short-sighted rent escalation clauses. Avoid tying increases in rent to the consumer price index, as this has proven to be very dangerous. If you have to include a provision for rent increases—and it would be unusual if you could avoid one—tie it to the long-term appreciation of the land and not the sporadic annual jumps in value that tend to be an appraiser's best guess. Keep in mind that you're renting the land, not offsetting the owner's loss in buying power due to inflation. Continued ownership of the land will do that, not your rental payments.

109. Lender Land Lease. This approach to financing can provide the incentive a lender needs to fund a project. The lender buys the land intended for development and leases it to the developer. Since the lender will be providing the first mortgage, there is not the degree of fear of subordination that is common with landowners who are leasing. The lender (maybe an insurance company) has full security, and the developer is, in effect, getting capital for land acquisition from the lender in addition to long-term financing, thus reducing the need for equity capital.

This technique is practically a joint venture approach to a sale lease-back that eliminates the intervening step of acquiring the land. Instead, you line up your lender and go into the project completely funded. The lender is really your backer and is investing in your ability to create value out of vacant land.

From the standpoint of long-term investment, the lender has an advantageous position through ownership of appreciating land that also produces current lease income. From your standpoint, the strategy is to develop the project, mortgage out, and generate sheltered income.

110. Leased Land Pyramid. Buying land subject to the improvements and existing financing and then leasing it back to the seller is an inflation protection investment. It is as good for small investors as it is for insurance companies. And it can be used as a rapid estate building-tool by simply varying the capitalization rate.

For example, if you can buy land for $100,000 and lease it back to the seller based on a capitalization rate of 10 percent, your rental income is $10,000 per year. At this point, you own the land and receive lease income. Next, exchange the land tax free based on a 5 percent capitalization rate. The $10,000 per year income has a value of $200,000 when capitalized at 5 percent (10,000 / 0.05 = 200,000). This is a matter of negotiation. It's also a matter of risk evaluation. This technique illustrates how you can build value into a general acquisition plan. There's a lot of truth to the statement that you make your money when you buy.

111. Sale Lease-Back as an Investment Opportunity. The sale and lease-back of successful business real estate is an excellent source of investment real estate. Under the right conditions, you can use this technique to bring property on the market.

Corporations often prefer to put capital in the business for expansion rather than having it tied up in real estate, which only sustains current operations. Every dollar of capital applied to the business serves to increase earnings, and having equity tied up in real estate can in some cases actually slow down corporate growth.

150

In the more fortunate situations, earnings will grow as fast as capital permits the company to expand. Approaching companies that may not have thought of this possibility is one way to locate investment property when there doesn't seem to be anything worthwhile on the market. With the competition for good investment real estate, techniques that embody an incentive for the seller can be invaluable.

The sale lease-back has a history of financing business expansion. From the standpoint of the company it is an investment capital-generating technique. Traditionally, the larger national corporations have put it to effective use, but it works equally well with established and growing small businesses.

112. Using a Lease to Gain Possession before Closing. Leasing has many applications that go beyond the conventional association with space rental. It is a fundamental real estate tool that can help build an acquisition structure in various situations.

For example, if mortgage rates are preventing the deal from closing, consider escrowing the down payment and leasing the property until the mortgage market eases. The seller will have a firm deal with cash in escrow to back it up plus lease income. You get use of the property now and time to arrange more satisfactory financing.

Leasing the property you want is a method of bridging the time gap that the reality of market conditions can present. The gap may even be years long when you lease with an option to buy. Textbook investments are the exception to actual real estate practice. When you want possession is not necessarily when requirements of the transaction will permit possession.

Chapter Ten

Acquisition with Options

Options hold a special place in real estate acquisition. They are rights to purchase without the obligation to perform associated with a conventional purchase agreement. In some highly leveraged cases, an option increases in value at a much greater percentage rate than would be possible with an outright purchase of the underlying property. An option also carries an implicit time advantage.

When you buy an option, you buy time to choose an action. If you choose not to acquire the property under option, it will expire at the agreed time with no consequence other than the forfeiture of its cost (if any).

The time you buy with an option can be put to varied uses. It's standard operating procedure to obtain a few months' option on land to run soil tests and check out the title and municipal requirements before making an all-out commitment to commercial development.

Options are also a useful speculation method. If you see progress moving toward an overlooked parcel of land, a well-negotiated option can put you in the position to profit. It's timing that makes the difference. If you move too soon and the buyers haven't reached the land before the option expires, you forfeit the option money. If you're planning to resell the option, you probably know the likely buyer even before you commit. In any event, options can take many forms and are adaptable to a number of different circumstances.

The basic option structure includes the price and terms for purchase of the property, the date, the right to transfer the option, and a provision allowing for extension of the option. Variations on this structure center on how the owner is compensated for granting the option, including the amount and timing of payment for the option. These negotiable terms can have a direct effect on the profit if you plan to resell the property or develop it.

Whether option costs should properly apply toward purchase or rest as separate payment for the time the property is off the market is negotiable. It depends which side of the table you're sitting on.

113. Interest Option. An interest option is one of the easier methods of paying for an option. Although it is not quite as good for the seller as other option structures, it is a logical way to calculate an option payment.

With this approach, the option consideration is an amount equal to the savings account interest on the value of the property for the period of the option. The details vary with circumstance. In some cases, the seller is paid only if the option is not exercised. If the option is exercised, the seller gets his price but no option consideration. Consequently, the option payment is compensation for loss of the sale and is made after the expiration date. If the option is exercised and the sale closes, there's no option payment because the seller reached the ultimate objective of selling the property.

It makes sense to tie an option payment to the property value even if the interest rate is a negotiable item. The owner may prefer that the rate be tied to the prime lending rate or the consumer price index. In any event, there's considerable flexibility when you have an idea of the components that make sense in arriving at a logical amount.

For example, it may make sense to the owner if you also agree to pay the property taxes prorated over the option period. Although it may be a minor amount for a few months' option in light of the total sales price, the appeal to a seller can edge the negotiations in your favor.

114. Effort Option. Option structures are as flexible as the people negotiating them. Look at what you want to accomplish and you'll likely see an option method. An effort option stipulates that you will obtain preliminary development plans and all necessary municipal approval within the option period at your expense. If you don't exercise the option, the plans, engineering studies, and other documentation, including any lease commitments you've obtained, become the property of the seller.

Since the value of land is to a large degree determined by its use, this approach transfers a degree of uncertainty to the seller by allowing you to verify the property's suitability with no cost for the time needed to do it.

If the property proves to be unsuitable for development, all you've lost is the cost of investigation. The seller is not paid for the cost of discovering that his property is inappropriate for the use you intend.

Turning over the results of your effort is simply a way to negotiate option control. The paperwork developed on a certain parcel has value even if it's only to eliminate a proposed use as part of the search to find the highest and best use. This option approach reduces your cost and covers a portion of the risk when there's a chance a particular location is not practical for your project.

115. Letter of Credit Option. A letter of credit can eliminate the need for cash while meeting the seller's requirement for option security. With this technique, you give the seller a letter of credit in the amount of the option consideration mutually agreed upon. If the option is not exercised, the seller collects on the letter of credit. If the option is exercised, the letter of credit is null and void.

The seller is fully protected in the event you don't complete the acquisition. You avoid the initial out-of-pocket cost of a standard option. With this approach, there is no additional payment to the seller above the property cost. The letter of credit is more than anything a guarantee that you are earnest in your plan to complete the purchase.

The cost to you, assuming the purchase is completed as planned, will probably be no more than interest charged by the bank for issuing the letter of credit. From a negotiation standpoint, though, you gain the same advantage you would by paying cash when the option is signed.

116. An Automatic Rolling Option with First Right of Refusal. This technique illustrates how an option can be combined with other provisions of an acquisition to meet specific project goals.

An automatic rolling option occurs when exercising one

option automatically establishes another option to acquire an adjacent parcel. The owner grants subsequent options as the prior ones are exercised. When exercising the initial option, you automatically roll it over to the adjacent parcel without additional payment.

The consideration for each option is built into the purchase of the previous parcel. It may not be necessary to increase the purchase price to obtain the option. The cash from your initial purchase and the probability of additional sales can be enough incentive to satisfy the owner.

An added benefit is that, although your legal option rolls only from one parcel to another at a time, there is a built-in first right of refusal for the entire tract, which may include dozens of separate parcels. Consequently, you tie up an entire project with only the expense of acquiring the parcels you need when you need them.

117. Continuing Option. A continuing option is set up by assigning the income from paper, which you own, to the owner of the property you are optioning. The property owner receives monthly income for a designated period, after which the option expires if not exercised.

This approach avoids a large up-front payment. Depending on the terms, it can provide the extended time necessary to sell the option for profit. It should be set up for a limited time, with the right to renew for another period equal to the first.

The purpose is to build in continuity. First, you establish an ongoing right by monthly option payments from the income-producing paper assigned to the property owner. The more he gets used to regular income, the less likely he will be to give it up. Second, you build in the right to renew or extend the option for a term equal to the original period. By providing for a continuing option, you build in profit potential when the objective is to speculate on the value of the property over an extended time period.

118. Increased Payment Option. This technique is designed to increase the option consideration in return for annual renewal. The initial agreement provides for increasing the payments to the seller if you choose to keep the option in force.

This is an incentive for the seller to grant a long-term option and allows you to tie up future appreciation early. For example, you can structure the payments so the seller receives $1,000 the first year, $2,000 the second, $3,000 the third year, but $5,000 the fourth year and $8,000 the fifth. The longer you control the property, the larger the payments to the seller.

It may also be appropriate to increase the purchase price as the option period progresses. If this requirement works into the deal, you may be able to offset it by applying part or all of the option payments to the purchase price. This can become a necessity toward the end of the option as payments increase.

119. Land Cost Option. Option consideration can be an excellent method for a seller to offset the costs of holding vacant land. With the right approach to negotiation, you can secure a relatively long-term option by simply paying the taxes on the property. If the owner knows the expenses are covered, and maybe a few other costs, negotiation of a long-term option can be smoother.

One of the drawbacks to investment in land that doesn't produce income is the cost of holding the property over a long period. Unfortunately, many land buyers don't discover this until they experience it firsthand.

A property owner who has been hit with this realization is a likely candidate for negotiation of an option that will soften the cost impact he's lived with for years. It's the unexpected that hurts the worst. A new paving or municipal utility assessment has brought more than one parcel of land on the market. If you size and time the option payment to cover the owner's cost, chances are you'll get his attention and have a good start toward acquiring the property.

120. Real Estate as Option Consideration. Deeding free-and-clear real estate or partial ownership shares can often be an effective option technique. This is a method of using the value of the land you have to acquire an option on additional real estate.

One of the best applications of this technique permits you to transfer value from lots that are away from areas being developed to property that is rapidly appreciating. The objective is to meet the basic requirement of sellers, which is to get a little extra consideration for granting the right to purchase.

A subdivision of lots in a mountain area that never quite got the public acceptance necessary for success can be a source for option consideration. Offering an owner one lot for a year's option to buy property you believe will appreciate can allow you to cash out of the mountain lots. Your option cost is essentially equal to the value of the lot. If you time it right, you'll be able to sell the option for more than the cost of the lot and make a profit by this creative use of property previously thought to have little value.

Chapter Eleven

Techniques for Building Value and Reducing Risk

There are always a few special real estate acquisition techniques that stand out as especially useful over the years. They may involve institution financing that you might not normally consider unless the deal is too good to pass up. Or, they may involve methods of creating value by dividing property into smaller units that sell at a higher percentage value. Some are different applications of familiar techniques. In addition, there are techniques that will help protect your property and give you a slight edge if trouble develops.

121. Pledge Additional Real Estate as Security. If you are borrowing to make a down payment and the bank wants more than your signature, offer to pledge other real estate as security. The pledge is recorded encumbering the property and is released when the loan is repaid.

122. Discount Buy-Back: When You Need Cash Immediately. If you need to raise cash in a hurry, consider selling your real estate at 50 percent of the market value, with an option to buy it back within three years for the actual market value on the day you sold it. Then, three years later, you buy the property back for a price based on the old value and either keep it or sell it at the appreciated value. Both the sales price today and the repurchase price three years later are below market value, yet everyone involved makes a profit. This approach requires that the property appreciate at a rate high enough to exceed the market value of three years ago. Vary the buy-back timing and the discount to fit market conditions.

123. Protect Level of Rental Income with an Adjustable Interest Rate. If you are acquiring apartments or other rental property and are concerned about possible vacancies, this approach may solve the problem. A simple way to protect against a drop in rental income is to decrease the interest rate on the seller's carry-back loan if vacancies occur. Then, if the market improves and the vacancies are filled, increase the interest rate to the original amount. This will help protect your cash flow and transfer part of the risk back to the seller.

124. Lower Risk and Increase Profits by Subordinating Debt Service to Cash Flow. When you are acquiring distressed property that the owner really wants out of, you can lower your risk and increase your profit potential by arranging for the debt service on the seller's carry-back financing, to be paid only after you have received a certain amount of cash flow.

The amount over the agreed cash flow would apply to interest and principal on the seller's equity. If the property has unexpected expenses that cut into your profit, the seller would sacrifice debt service payments to protect your cash flow. The seller is guaranteeing the property's profitability by subordinating the debt service payments to your cash flow.

125. When Money Is a Problem, Buy with Paper but Cash Out the Seller. If you have no cash but the seller wants cash, raise the purchase price to offset a discount on the second mortgage. Assume the first mortgage and give the seller a second mortgage, which is then discounted and sold to get the cash needed for the down payment. The increase in the purchase price offsets the discount necessary to sell the second for cash.

126. Make an Installment Down Payment. You can acquire property on an installment basis by arranging with the seller to pay a certain amount of cash into a special escrow account until the down payment amount is made. This approach involves setting up a special agreement that establishes a closing when the down payment amount is paid in full.

127. Minimize Your Risk by Making Price Contingent on

159

Resale. If you are acquiring real estate for resale and the seller doesn't mind sharing the risk and the possibility of a higher profit, set a sliding scale for the purchase price that establishes a profit for you and a higher price for the seller if you succeed. The seller's trust in your ability to get a higher sales price can result in acquisition terms for you that are virtually without risk.

128. Protect Your Partnership Investment with a Buy-Sell Agreement. If you are acquiring property in partnership, be sure to establish a buy-sell agreement with the other partners. The agreement should cover the transfer of ownership and management in the event of the death of one of the partners. It should also set up a buyout procedure if the partners can't get along in the decision-making process.

129. When You Are Uncertain, Set Up a Buy-Back Agreement. If you are uneasy about the property you are acquiring, set up an agreement with the seller to buy the property back within a limited time period. For example, the agreement might require the seller to buy the property back within three months if you are dissatisfied for any reason.

130. Avoid Foreclosure by Entering into a Joint Venture with Notes. If an owner is in danger of losing his equity in vacant land because of an inability to make the payments, a joint venture may solve the problem. If the debt service payment is large, an acquisition in partnership by several individuals who are each easily capable of making their portion of the land payment is the first step. The seller's equity could then be purchased with several personal notes from the individual partners to spread the risk.

131. Obtain a Discount in Exchange for a Large Cash Payment. If you are planning to pay off a privately held mortgage, don't overlook the possibility of acquiring additional equity that may be available for the asking. If you catch the mortgage holder at the right time, she may give you a discount to receive a large and unexpected cash payment in exchange for the discount before you refinance. Of course, this approach is a matter of negotiation.

132. What to Do When a Note Is Due and There Is No Cash.
What can you do when a note is due and there's no cash to make
the payment? Try negotiating an extension and, as an incentive,
paying the note-holder a late charge.

If the lender is worried that you may not be able to pay the
note at the end of the extension, offer additional security and an
increase in the interest rate. The objective is to increase the
benefits to the holder of the note as consideration for an extension
or, if possible, a change in the terms of the note.

*133. Maximize Leverage with Subordination to Construction
Financing.* If you're planning to acquire vacant land for
development and want to maximize leverage, negotiate
subordination of the seller's interest to construction financing.

This will allow you to build without paying off the land loan
until construction is complete and the permanent financing is in
place. This approach can work to maximum benefit when it is used
with a mortgage-out strategy.

134. Reduce the Down Payment with a Broker Loan. If you
have trouble meeting the cash requirement for a down payment,
the brokers involved may be a source of financing. This approach
can be accomplished with the commissions or other funds the
brokers may have available for investment at a high interest rate. It
can be especially attractive to brokers with high incomes who
would benefit from a readily available investment.

*135. Refinance Property During Acquisition by Substituting
Collateral While Preserving Installment Reporting.* Refinancing
property during acquisition can be a problem if the holder of the
seller's original financing (the existing first mortgage) will not
accept an early payoff because she wants to maintain installment
reporting. The solution is to leave the note undisturbed but
substitute different security.

A mortgage on different real estate or even a certificate of
deposit could be used. This approach allows the property to be
freed for the new financing, but the note remains untouched,
protecting the original installment reporting for the note-holder
(from whom the current seller originally bought the property).

136. Use an Inheritance Pledge to Facilitate Acquisition. If you have an inheritance that is established, it can be a help to you in acquiring real estate. Buy the real estate you want on a note secured by the inheritance. The holder of the note would get the first right to the proceeds at settlement of the estate. You get the real estate now, and the seller gets security.

137. Use an Irrevocable Trust as Security. If you have an irrevocable trust that is producing a very low return on equity that could be increased through real estate investment, you may be able to use it as security. The income from the trust could be pledged to secure a personal note or be diverted to actually amortize an acquisition note.

138. Put Off Making Large Payments by Reversing the Interest. By structuring an acquisition with separate notes that are due annually, you can place the high interest payments at the end of the amortization term rather than at the beginning. One note is paid, plus accrued interest, at the end of each 12-month period.

Consequently, the first note bears one year's interest, the fifth year's note bears five years' interest, and the twentieth bears 20 years' interest.

One mortgage is used to secure all the notes. This places the burden of making large payments in the later years. The seller can defer ordinary income in the earlier years of the sale.

139. Protect the Interest with a Noncompetition Agreement. Competition is a major factor in real estate investments. If you are acquiring property from a developer who might go into competition with you, consider requiring a noncompetition agreement.

The agreement should state that the seller will not build a competing project within, for example, a three-mile radius of the property you are acquiring for a three-year period. In exchange for this agreement, the seller may require a fee, which could be offset by lowering the sales price.

140. Lower the Loan Balance by Increasing the Interest.

Market value of real estate is sometimes lower than the loan balances as a result of vandalism, fire, or market conditions. The key element to this solution is low interest on the original loans. If that is the case, negotiate a reduction in the outstanding loan balance, provided the monthly payments remain the same. The owner of the loan will receive the same in gross income and total loan payments, but a greater percentage of the income from the debt service will be interest income. The benefit is that the loan balance is reduced to a level that is more reasonable in relation to the reduced market value of the property, but the note-holder gets the same total cash flow.

141. Buy Paper at a Discount and Trade at Face Value. One of the best estate-building techniques is to buy paper at a discount and, with careful negotiation, use it as the down payment to acquire real estate. You can pick up immediate profit while moving from a declining debt investment (paper) to an appreciating equity investment (real estate).

142. Assign the Payments. Don't Trade the Paper. Rather than conveying ownership of a note as down payment, establish an escrow agreement that assigns the payments from the note to the seller as security for a new note with identical terms.

The seller will receive the total income from the new note as consideration for the down payment. The original note remains intact and provides security for the transaction.

143. Always Try for a Release Clause to Lower Your Risk. If you are buying land, always try to negotiate the release of an appropriate percentage of the total as you reduce the loan principal. Releases often prove to be of special importance in determining the value of the property in the future. Release clauses allow you to avoid the necessity of paying off the entire debt balance before getting a development loan. If for some reason things turn for the worse, you will have part of the property free and clear if you have to default on the balance of the loan. Release clauses protect part of your equity.

144. Certificate of Appreciation Participation. If you are trapped in a property that is worth less than the loan value (under water) this technique is worth trying. Ask the lender to reduce the amount of the loan to the actual market value of the property and lower the interest and payments in exchange for participation in future appreciation of the property as the real estate cycle turns. The amount of participation would equal the amount of reduction in the loan balance, with a factor for actual appreciation. For example, a percentage of the loan reduction in relation to the original loan amount could form the basis to allocate the appreciation between the equity and debt owners. The Appreciation Participation Agreement would be recorded as a lien against the property that is due on sale, with provisions to participate in future refinancing proceeds.

145. The Most Important Technique. Always use a competent real estate attorney. For the most part, these techniques involve contract law and require a skilled, specialized real estate attorney, preferably one with a background in tax law. Why is this a technique? Because an experienced real estate attorney can provide refinements that enhance a transaction and more than pay for the fees involved. Besides, staying out of trouble is the foundation of success.

Chapter Twelve

Real Estate Exchange Techniques

There are many reasons to exchange real estate. The obvious one is to avoid loss of equity to income tax. Nontaxable exchange under the provisions of Section 1031 of the Internal Revenue Code is one of the few real tax shelters remaining for real estate investors. It allows the exchange of like-kind property (all real estate) that is held for investment or use in trade or business. It does not include property used as a personal residence, which has its own beneficial tax advantages.

The Tax Reform Act of 1986 established a legislated provision for the multiparty exchange, which had until then been based solely on case law and revenue rulings. Formerly known as the Starker exchange, named after a court case, this procedure is now referred to as a "deferred exchange" in the regulations. It allows transfer of property and replacement under specific conditions outlined in IRS Publication 544. You may transfer property and replace it if:

1. Replacement property is designated within 45 days from transfer;

2. Replacement property is received within 180 days of transfer or the due date plus extensions of the tax return for year of transfer; and

3. Cash from the initial transfer is restricted by agreement and held by a third party that prevents actual or constructive receipt (legal right) by the taxpayer.

This safe harbor provision has spawned a new industry of companies that provide documentation and hold money to facilitate nontaxable exchanges. Title companies have also provided this service.

If you are considering an exchange, the first calculation should be by your accountant to determine if the tax due on sale warrants the cost of completing an exchange. Once you have that in hand, here are a few techniques to consider.

146. A Basic Two-Party Exchange. Despite the complexity of the IRS provisions, simple exchanges are still possible. If you find property you want and the owner is willing to take your property, you have a meeting of the minds for a two-party exchange. Any tax due will be limited to the boot used to balance equities. Boot is what kicks the deal to completion and can involve a horse or cash or any property that is not like kind.

A hidden danger in any exchange is relief from mortgage debt, which is considered taxable boot. This means that if you have a realized gain, it will be recognized to the extent that the mortgage you dispose of is more than the mortgage you assume. The best way is to move up to a larger property value with a larger mortgage. The alternative may still be desirable but don't let mortgage relief be a surprise.

It is likely in a two-party exchange that the equities will not balance and one of the parties will give and one will get boot. This does not jeopardize the portion of the exchange that is nontaxable. A partially taxable exchange is acceptable to the IRS.

147. Pyramiding Real Estate by Exchanging. Pyramiding is a process of acquiring real estate of increasingly greater value by nontaxable exchange. Pyramid refers to the movement of ownership from lower to higher total value. Each exchange is a move up. The objective is to use the tax-free benefit to increase the compounding effect of equity appreciation. By making a nontaxable exchange a part of your acquisition program, the portion of equity that would go to payment of tax is used to acquire more real estate.

Pyramiding is effective because of the equity saved by exchanging. But if you can acquire real estate below market value or improve it in ways that increase its value, you will be that much further ahead.

Normally, pyramiding is a gradual process that occurs over a period of years. One fortunate investor began the process by acquiring a rental duplex in a university area on the verge of rapid expansion. Fortunately, the seller didn't want a lot of cash, so the investor was able to buy the property for $500 down. Over the next five years, due to increased rents, unusually rapid appreciation in real estate values, and loan amortization, the duplex equity increased to $10,000.

The leverage of a very low down payment got him off to the right start. When the opportunity came to step up by exchange, he was ready. The duplex was exchanged tax free for a 12-unit apartment complex, which, after two years of patient ownership, resulted in a significant increase in total benefits. The new property, because of its size, provided larger value appreciation, greater debt reduction (equity build-up), and a much higher net cash flow than the duplex would ever have been able to produce.

148. Exchanging for Property with Faster Appreciation. An exchange for greater appreciation is based on the reasoning that if you are holding property for increase in incremental value, it should be appreciating as fast as possible. If your investment real estate is located in an area that is going downhill or not appreciating at the rate you think it should, an exchange may solve the problem. Keeping in mind that real estate is a vehicle for reaching broader personal goals, look at the sections of your city to determine the path of progress. The direction of population growth and new building indicates where the fastest appreciation is and the area to find exchange property.

To apply this strategy, establish an appreciation trend by geographic area. Which areas are declining? Which are developing? Where is property most in demand? Which type is in demand in a given area; i.e., improved property, vacant land, residential rental, or commercial? Then compare your property and the area it's in to what's available in other areas. There's no limit to the size of the area for consideration—block, subdivision, quadrant, city, state, climatic region. Why not consider as many possibilities as you feel comfortable with?

One investor moved his holdings in a series of exchanges from a slum in a large city to a small mining town, which later boomed due to the demand for energy. It took patience, but the potential was recognized before the first step, and within three years, the plan paid off.

If the investment objective is maximum appreciation, well-planned exchanges can move your ownership to locations that meet the goal without the tax.

149. Exchange for Loan Value. Exchanging can result in a significant increase in return on equity. But to increase the percentage of return on equity, it is sometimes necessary to refinance, thus reducing the relative amount of equity.

Unfortunately, there are certain types of properties that lending institutions won't make loans on, and there are properties they will loan on but shouldn't. In any event, an exchange for real estate that is acceptable for loan purposes can generate cash, increase percentage return on equity, and result in a more secure investment.

To analyze this possibility, establish the property's current return on equity. What is it compared to what it could be? Then, can it be refinanced—just what is the loan value: 70 percent, 75 percent, 80 percent, or nothing? Maybe the age, location, and condition eliminate the possibility of refinancing. Or is it that loans aren't available for commercial property and an exchange into residential income will solve the problem? When potential exchange property is found, establish its loan value and make sure a loan will be possible before committing yourself to the transaction.

In one case, an investor exchanged free and clear commercial rental property with no loan value for a free and clear apartment complex. His basis was transferred from the commercial property to the apartments. After the transaction closed, he financed the apartments, increasing the percentage return on equity. He then reinvested the tax-free loan funds and increased the total size of his real estate portfolio.

150. Exchange for Property with a Lower Debt Service Payment. Exchanging for property with lower debt payments can solve a number of problems while increasing equity return. High interest rates, short-term loans, and balloon payments tend to reduce return. Acquiring property with equal equity and expenses but lower loan payments automatically increases return on equity.

This can be accomplished by locating property with established loans or by negotiating a carry-back loan with a lower interest rate and generally favorable terms not possible with conventional financing. But when this type of exchange is called for, return on equity is often not the major consideration. An investor saddled with loan payments that the property doesn't support can be faced with more of a personal than an investment problem. This is a serious issue in situations involving vacant land payments that cut into discretionary income.

One of the most effective applications of this exchange strategy is obtaining relief from vacant land payments. In one case, an investor had a substantial equity in 10 acres that was not producing income. Due to changes in his job situation, the large land payments became prohibitive and he was in danger of foreclosure. By structuring an exchange for income property, he not only protected the land equity but also received cash flow equal to the amount of the former land payments.

Bonus Section: Seven Exchange Techniques

151. Exchange a Nonproductive Equity for Income. Return on equity can take a real jump when land is traded for income-producing real estate. Farmers have experienced this benefit when faced with the fact that certain land is more valuable as a subdivision than as a farm.

A 640-acre farm purchased 30 years ago at $100 per acre and valued today at $1,000 an acre is a real retirement asset. The farm equity of $640,000 can produce significant annual income when exchanged for income-producing real estate. What better way to retire than with a larger income than could be earned by farming and at the same time leveraging the transaction to increase the estate size?

The exchange strategy applies equally well for all land owners, including ranchers, investors, and city lot owners. The objective is to receive maximum return on appreciated equity in today's dollars without the diminishing effect of paying tax on a sale.

152. Exchanging to Solve Problems and Secure Benefits That Go Beyond Tax and Investment Considerations. The benefits available through exchanging are not limited to tax and investment considerations. Exchanging plays a large part in solving problems and meeting personal objectives in ways not possible by selling. These are the situations that broaden the meaning of value and separate it from price. The distinction between value and price is created by the effect of the transaction on the owner. With problem real estate, the value of the exchange to the owner psychologically may far exceed the market value of the property. To establish the price of real estate without considering the value of a specific transaction to the owner is an incomplete analysis. Price is one factor contributing to value, but the emotional effect of an exchange on the owner may be more important and must ultimately figure in the decision to go ahead with a specific transaction.

Putting people before property is essential to good judgment in any transaction. Opportunities to secure benefits are almost unending in real estate. Real estate is a means to an end—a vehicle to carry people to relatively better circumstances. The value of real estate is in what it can do for people. A dollar price established arbitrarily at some passing moment is a shot in the dark at a fixed value. At best, a price set out of context from an owner is a hollow abstraction. Only by introducing real people with needs, desires, and unique objectives can value be established. No doubt that is why real estate negotiation is so often a difficult process. Value is in the use of the property to a living person and a concept completely separate from price.

Going one step further to define real estate value in terms of what it can do for you is the only way to protect yourself from making the wrong decision. It seems that more people kick themselves for not making an acquisition at what seemed a high price at the time than those who do make such an acquisition.

Don't confuse value with price. Value is where the real estate vehicle will take you as an individual. Price is someone else's shot in the dark at dollars. Not making a move because the price set by some stranger seems "too high (or if you're selling, too low) for today's market" can result in a loss of real, personally measurable value. Money is only an abstraction; people are real, and the only determinant of value.

153. Consolidation of Assets. Management demands of real estate scattered over a large geographic area can become an energy drain. Although rental houses and duplexes acquired through the years may represent hard-earned equity, the effect on health and lifestyle of management can overshadow the investment benefits. Consolidation of several properties into one large complex can eliminate management demands without loss of equity to tax.

The primary benefit of a consolidation exchange is management centralization. A pyramiding step-up in overall value can also be a natural by-product. And the entire process can be tax free.

In making this strategy work, it is reasonable to assume that the owner of a large income property wouldn't want several scattered houses and duplexes any more than the person disposing of them. The solution is to find a wholesale buyer for the scattered property or, if practical, individual buyers to buy the houses out of escrow. This approach sets up a multiparty or deferred transaction, resulting in a nontaxable exchange for the consolidating taxpayer, a sale for the larger income property owner, and a purchase for the new owner(s) of the houses and duplexes.

154. Arrange a Transaction Not Otherwise Possible. An exchange is sometimes the only way to complete a real estate transaction. For example, take the expansion necessitated by a successful business. The business must have a specific parcel of real estate, which the owner refuses to sell because of the tax consequences. This is a natural exchange opportunity. Multiparty exchanges probably solve more acquisition problems of this type than any other technique. This problem normally arises when the business needs the property for expansion and the owner can't afford to sell because of taxes.

The solution is the standard multiparty exchange in which the business agrees to acquire real estate designated by the owner and exchange it for the desired parcel. There's no other way the transaction can go through. The business must have the property. But the property owner refuses to accept the tax consequences of a sale. Both objectives are met in an exchange. The business owns the property it needs, and the taxpayer acquires other real estate with possibly more potential and income.

155. Exchange for Investment Property That Is Easier to Sell.

171

Exchanging property that is difficult to sell for a number of rental houses, duplexes, and triplexes can increase the ease of a sale because of the smaller units.

This strategy involves completing the exchange and holding the more saleable property for income or investment. When the property has appreciated to the investment objective over a reasonable period of time, sell it.

The distinction between this procedure and exchanging with a contingent cash takeout is that the property received is not sold at closing. It is held for investment (not sale) and sold when the market is right for taking profit. Being involved in a multiparty exchange as the supplier of exchange property who receives cash at closing is one transaction with a capital gain sale. But closing an exchange and later selling the real estate received results in two transactions. Therefore, care must be taken to avoid any implication that the property acquired in the exchange was held for sale rather than investment.

156. Exchange for New Circumstances. If you want to retain an investment in real estate but need a change in lifestyle, consider exchanging. For example, retirement and travel plans don't mix with the management demands of rental property. An exchange for well-located land can eliminate the management problems and provide other benefits.

This situation occurred with a retiring civil service worker who acquired a number of older rentals over the years. Although he had sizeable equity, the net income from the 10 rental houses was small and not worth foregoing travel plans.

The solution was to stay in real estate ownership but get out of rentals; that is, exchange circumstances. If you accept the concept that real estate is a vehicle to reach personal objectives, it follows that if the objectives change, it may be necessary to change vehicles. This is exactly what happened with the retired civil service worker.

He had retirement income and didn't need the small amount contributed by his rentals. But what he did want was the stability and security of a well-placed real estate investment. He got that by exchanging the rental houses for acreage located about five years away from the major residential growth of the city. Returning from five years of travel would place him in a position to sell the land at long-term capital gains estimated to be larger than that anticipated from his rentals. More importantly, he eliminated management responsibility without sacrificing equity and was able to travel with peace of mind.

157. Intrinsic Benefits of Exchanging. There are several benefits that follow naturally from exchanging. Although they are minor compared to the sometimes tremendous tax savings and increases in equity return, they deserve mentioning.

Aside from the specific tax or business objectives, an exchange often results in a general change in the circumstances surrounding an owner's life. Transferring real estate can solve a whole set of personal problems. For example, high monthly land payments that are beyond the financial capacity of the owner have more than once strained family relations. What was once a long-term investment may become a symbol of bad judgment or a deal in which you "got taken." When this type of thinking starts, it's time to exchange.

Lifetime estate conservation is another benefit inherent in the nontaxable exchange. If lifetime estate conservation is carried to its logical extreme, you can acquire real estate and continue to exchange throughout life without ever selling. You could pyramid equity on equity, never paying tax. Transaction after transaction can be made without one cent lost to tax, which is a very efficient way to build an estate.

Making an exchange also automatically eliminates the decision of where to invest funds—a decision that is difficult for some to make. In a tax-free exchange, there's no problem of what to do with money. The decision is made by the nature of the transaction. Equity is not converted to money; it stays in real estate.

All of the tax, investment, business, and other exchange benefits can appear separately and in combination in any given transaction. In fact, the complexity of some exchanges tends to obscure the advantages until it's all over.

Exchanging involves complex and often conflicting negotiation. To fit the puzzle of each principal's objectives together in one closed transaction requires a tradeoff of desires and a balance of objectives often reached by a combination of acquisition techniques. The seemingly unending list of real estate acquisition and financing techniques may at first glance seem unrelated to exchanging. But an exchange is a tax and economic structure held together by these very techniques. They provide the means to trade the principals' often conflicting objectives and balance the transaction. The techniques in this book are designed for daily reference to help you put deals together.

It's difficult to imagine how complicated a transaction can become until you get into it. To overcome the complexity, it is essential to have principals who want the exchange to go through. Without everyone pulling together in a spirit of give and take, few exchanges would ever close.

###